QTLS

Assessing Learning
in the Lifelong Learning Sector

Assessing Learning
in the Lifelong Learning Sector

Third edition

Jonathan Tummons

LearningMatters

First published in 2005 by Learning Matters Ltd
Reprinted in 2006
Second edition published in 2007
Reprinted in 2007
Reprinted in 2008
Reprinted in 2009
Reprinted in 2010
Third edition published in 2011

British Library Cataloguing in Publication Data
A CIP record for this book is available from the British Library.

ISBN: 978 0 85725 268 5

This book is also available in the following ebook formats:
Adobe ebook ISBN: 978 0 85725 270 8
EPUB ebook: ISBN: 978 0 85725 269 2
Kindle ISBN: 978 0 85725 271 5

Cover design by Topics – The Creative Partnership
Project management by Deer Park Productions, Tavistock
Typeset by PDQ Typesetting Ltd, Newcastle-under-Lyme
Printed and bound by Bell & Bain Ltd, Glasgow

Learning Matters Ltd
20 Cathedral Yard
Exeter EX1 1HB
Tel: 01392 215560
info@learningmatters.co.uk
www.learningmatters.co.uk

MIX
Paper from
responsible sources
FSC® C007785

Contents

The author

Jonathan Tummons has worked in higher education since 1995. He took up a post as senior lecturer in education at Teesside University in 2009 after six years as a lecturer in teacher education in the FE sector. As a consultant, he has contributed to programmes for schools broadcast by Channel 4. Jonathan is currently completing an ESRC-funded PhD at the University of Lancaster, researching the assessment of trainee teachers in the learning and skills sector.

Acknowledgements

Every effort has been made to trace the copyright holders and to obtain their permission for the use of copyright material. The publisher and author will gladly receive information enabling them to rectify any error or omission in subsequent editions.

The author and publisher would like to thank the following for permission to reproduce copyright material.

HMSO
Edexcel
The Tavistock Institute
Taylor & Francis Group

The author would like to acknowledge the contributions made by the following people, in different places at different times: Neil Arnott, John Aston, Jocelyn Brooks, Malcolm Chase, Roy Fisher, David Lamburn, Jayne Moore, David Neve, Lynne Paxton, Peter Rycraft, Eileen Shaw, students at Yorkshire Coast College of Further and Higher Education, particularly Julie Mayo and Jenny Stamford, students at York College. And especially, as always, Jo.

A note on the third edition
Several people have helped develop both my thinking and my practice since the first edition of this book was written, and I would like to acknowledge them here. So, thanks to: Liz Atkins, Eleanor Glynn, Ewan Ingleby, Kevin Orr, Gillian Rodgers, Gustav Pavlov and Sharon Powell.

Introduction

This book is intended to help all those who are currently working towards a teaching qualification accredited by Lifelong Learning UK (LLUK). You may already be working as a teacher or trainer in a Further Education college, and studying for your professional quali-fications on a part-time, in-service basis. Alternatively, you may be studying for your qualification on a full-time basis and may be about to embark on, or already engaged on, a teaching placement. You may be employed, or seeking employment, as a tutor in adult or community education, provided by a local education authority or by organisations such as the Workers' Educational Association (WEA). You may be working as a trainer or instructor in the health sector, or in the police or fire services. These varied contexts are all covered by the LLUK standards and practitioners in these areas are all eligible for LLUK accreditation.

This is not a theoretical book. There are many aspects of current assessment practice that have inspired research and exploration but this level of theoretical investigation is outside the scope of this book. However, there are occasions when a focus on current research is desirable and the references provided will allow those with a taste for theory to explore further.

This book aims to help trainee teachers to explore the key principles and practices in assessment and to encourage them to reflect on the ideas and issues that are raised. An investigation of the role of reflective practice within the teacher-training curriculum is also beyond the scope of this book, but the key principle of blending theory with practice under-pins both. This book is intended to provoke action as well as thought. The activities are supported by case studies that are composites of real-life experiences that I have encoun-tered. They are designed to facilitate the application of the ideas and issues discussed in the real world of the teacher or trainer.

Meeting the National Occupational Standards

From 1 January 2005 a new organisation, Lifelong Learning UK (LLUK), began operating as the body responsible for – among other things – the professional development of all employ-ees in the field of lifelong learning. LLUK was responsible for the occupational standards that appear in this book (at the beginning of each chapter) until early in 2011, when responsibility for the standards – and the current debates over how these might be reformed – was transferred to the Learning and Skills Improvement Service (LSIS).

How to use this book

This book may be read from cover to cover or on a chapter-by-chapter basis. Each chapter is designed so that it can be read in isolation, although references to topics covered in other chapters will be found from time to time.

Within each chapter, the reader will find a number of features that are designed to engage the reader, and provoke an active response to the ideas and themes that are covered. **Objectives** at the start of each chapter set the scene, and then the appropriate **LLUK profes-**

sional standards for that chapter are listed. In many places, an **activity** will be found. These activities have been designed to facilitate the practical application of some of the issues covered. Similarly, a range of **focus** activities is also included. Some of the focus activities are designed to draw attention to certain details; others are designed to stimulate **reflection** and debate; and some are designed to draw attention to some current and recent debates in educational **theory** and research, as they relate to professionalism. The case studies and real-life examples that are to be found in this book are drawn from a variety of different teaching and training contexts, as a reflection of the diversity of the learning and skills sector as a whole. Finally, each chapter finishes with suggestions for what to do next. A set of three **branching options** allows you to consolidate what you have learnt and to stretch your skills and understanding. A small number of sources, books, journal articles and websites are recommended at the end of each chapter. These lists are by no means exhaustive. Featured items have been chosen because of their suitability and value for use and study by trainee teachers in the learning and skills sector.

It is assumed that learning is facilitated if the learner's own experiences can be drawn on and valued. And so, throughout this book, readers will be asked to think about their own experiences, both as a student as well as a tutor or trainee tutor. It is also assumed that learning is facilitated through reflective practice, the application of ideas to practice and the evaluation of practice at a later time. Of course people learn and study in different ways. The activities in this book have been designed for those readers who enjoy actively engaging with what they read, but they are not compulsory: those with a taste for the theoretical can return to the activities at a later date, or may prefer to pursue the ideas for further reading at the end of some of the chapters.

As well as opening up a range of issues and themes for discussion and reflection, this book also contains practical tips and strategies that could have a more immediate application, or provide inspiration, within the teaching and training practices of readers. Once again, these ideas are by no means exhaustive, nor will they prove applicable in every teaching context. For a wider range of strategies and hints, further reading is recommended.

Learning, and reading this book

My own research is focused on how trainee teachers in the learning and skills sector make sense of the assessment requirements that they have to meet whilst studying for their teacher training qualifications. From this perspective, as well as from my perspective as a teacher educator, I have radically changed my own ideas about what I think learning is, and how it can be made to happen. This book is not an appropriate venue for me to set forth my own views, but one or two comments are, I feel, necessary. Firstly, a general point: I think that learning can happen in all kinds of places and at all kinds of times, and it never really stops. Learning happens as a consequence of our social actions: talking to colleagues or friends; going to work; finding ways to deal with dilemmas that we have not encountered before. In this book, I have tried to set out a number of themes and ideas, and to situate them firmly within the working lives of tutors.

Secondly, a more specific point: I think that language needs to be used carefully. There is a lot of jargon in teacher education and despite my efforts and assurances, many of the trainees with whom I have worked still resist it. In this book, I have tried to cut the use of jargon to a minimum. There is a place for it: the right words can say in a small amount of space what might otherwise take a long time. There are also, in teacher education, a number of books and articles that are sometimes a little forbidding to the reader, especially to those for whom teacher training is a first experience of higher education. I have tried to keep this reader in mind, whilst at the same time providing sufficient depth for the more academically experienced reader.

I am always happy to hear from trainee teachers about my writing or my research and to receive offers from trainees who would be willing to help. My email address is j.tummons@tees.ac.uk.

1
Thinking about assessment

Introduction

This chapter looks at assessment in general terms: what it is, why we do it, when we do it and who is involved in the assessment process. Although some of these issues relate to assessment in its broadest educational sense, this chapter focuses on assessment principles and practice in the further education sector. It concludes with a brief consideration of the importance of reviewing and reflecting on our assessment practice as teachers in further education, with reference to the national occupational standards that currently support our work.

> **PRACTICAL TASK** PRACTICAL TASK PRACTICAL TASK PRACTICAL TASK PRACTICAL TASK
>
> Before reading on, spend a few moments thinking about assessment. What do you think the assessment process actually is? Why is it so important?

What is assessment?

Assessment is a word that can have several meanings. Within the world of education and training, it equates to testing: if a learner is being assessed, then he or she is being tested. Normally, this test would be carried out to discover whether or not the learner could perform a specified task in a workshop, or to judge the extent to which the learner has mastered a new skill or a new body of theoretical knowledge. Educational assessment, as we shall see, can happen at different times and in different places. But the fundamentals that underpin the process remain the same. On the one hand, there is the learner, who has been practising her new computer skills or her newly acquired Italian language skills. On the other hand, there is the teacher or trainer, who is going to assess the extent to which the learner can now use those skills to create a web-page or to have a conversation in Italian without needing to look words up in a dictionary.

Why do we assess?

You might think that this is a rather odd question. After all, if we are going to be working as teachers or trainers in the Lifelong Learning sector, then assessment will be a permanent and unavoidable aspect of our professional role. However, this is a question that deserves some attention. The place of assessment in all its forms (and there are lots of ways in which assessment is carried out, as we shall see) is accepted without question in schools, colleges and universities throughout the country. And while the history of education goes back hundreds (if not thousands) of years, trying to discover the historic roots of assessment may not be a straightforward exercise. People have been teaching or training other people how to do things for a very long time: nowadays most of our attention is focused on the teaching and learning that takes place in formal educational institutions, which is where FE colleges enter the picture.

Like education as a whole, the sector has changed dramatically over recent years. The way that colleges are run, the mechanisms for funding education and training provision, the growth of a more business-like ethos, even the changing nature of professional qualifications for tutors: in all these areas, and more, colleges have both changed and been changed. There are several reasons for this. Successive governments have taken an interest in education and implemented changes of various kinds over the years, encouraging more people to stay in education for longer, or to return to education and training later in life. Changes in technology and business have led to the growth of new kinds of educational provision. Changes in social attitudes have allowed more people, from broader social and economic backgrounds, to participate in education for longer. Changing economic conditions have led to a need for more people to be better qualified. And lastly, changing educational methods have led to the growth of education and training not only in colleges, but also in the workplace, in industry and increasingly via the Internet.

In short, we now have more people taking part in education and training in more places, studying more subjects, over more varied periods of time, than ever before. And a lot of this variety can be found in the sector, which embodies diversity: academic and vocational programmes; technical and professional programmes; full-time and part-time programmes; daytime and evening programmes. Even the age-range of the people who attend colleges is diversifying. As well as so-called 'mainstream' learners aged between 16 and 19, FE colleges also provide a range of courses for younger learners aged between 14 and 16 (who may be studying towards a Diploma), and for adult learners as well (on access to HE courses, or work-based learning courses, for example).

With such a variety of learners and courses, it is no surprise that there is also a great deal of variety in assessment practice as well. Learners write essays, complete practical assignments, create artwork, compile portfolios of evidence and organise public performances. They are assessed in seminar rooms, workshops, libraries and public places. Sometimes, these assessments are highly individualised, and designed by their tutor. At other times, learners from across the country will be completing similar if not identical assessment activities, perhaps at the same time. Despite this variety, however, the fundamental reasons why the assessment process has to happen are the same.

With assessment we can:

1. find out if learning has taken place;
2. diagnose learners' needs;
3. provide public acknowledgement and certification of learning;
4. allow processes of selection to be carried out;
5. provide a way to evaluate learning programmes;
6. motivate and encourage learners.

REFLECTIVE TASK

Drawing on these six reasons for assessment, reflect on the different experiences of assessment that you have had at different stages in your educational life. Make a brief note of all the times that you were assessed, and think about why you think that each stage of assessment was necessary.

Now think about the programme of teacher training you are currently undertaking. Using the various course handbooks, handouts and other course documents that you have received, write a list of all the assessment activities that you will need to complete during the programme. Returning to the list, reflect on the extent to which these six reasons for assessment support the assessments that you will carry out during your teacher training course.

As we look at each of these six issues in turn, consider the extent to which each issue is important and relevant in the curriculum area within which you teach or train. If you are studying for your teaching qualification on a part-time in-service programme, reflect on your current teaching experience. If you are studying on a full-time course, your experience on teaching placement will be valuable: talk to other teachers, or to your mentor.

1. Finding out if learning has taken place

The most straightforward answer to the question 'what is education and training for?' must be 'to teach people new skills, abilities and bodies of knowledge'. The reasons why we do this are rather more complicated, and draw on political, economic and philosophical arguments that are beyond the scope of this book. But our first question and answer can stand. Having established this as the main purpose of education and training, the need for assessment is obvious. Assessment, in all its many forms, is the process by which it is possible to find out the extent to which learning has taken place. Have the trainees acquired the new skills that they have been shown by their instructor and that they have been practising in the workshop? Have the learners in a language class been able to remember the vocabulary that they were asked to study and memorise, and can they use it in conversation? This is assessment of learning and, together with assessment for learning, is discussed in depth in Chapter 3.

There are many theories regarding learning – what it is, how it happens and what conditions are needed for learning to take place are just some of the questions that are mulled over by researchers and writers. And there are as many questions regarding knowledge and understanding: are there different types of knowledge? How is knowledge acquired? It is important to consider different ideas such as these, and different programmes for trainee further education lecturers include theories of learning in the curriculum. For the purposes of this book, learning is taken to be: the acquisition or enhancement of new knowledge, skill, ability or understanding and the ability to use or apply this knowledge, skill, ability or understanding after the college course or programme of study is over.

Measuring the learning that has taken place will vary according to the type of course being studied. Methods of assessment are explored in more detail in Chapter 5. For now, it is important to remember that however the assessment is carried out, the requirement to measure the learning that has taken place remains the same. From this point, we can explore other reasons why assessment is necessary.

2. Diagnosing learners' needs

If the process of assessment tells the tutor, or the institution where the tutor works, that learning has not yet taken place, then a number of different issues arise. It is always pleasant to be able to tell learners that they have passed an assignment or an examination; it is more difficult to tell them that they have failed an examination, or have submitted an assignment that is not of a sufficient standard to pass and so needs to be done again. It may simply be the case that the learner needs to prepare more thoroughly and practise more carefully before the next assessment is due. Careful feedback (as discussed in Chapter 6) will give that learner the extra guidance they need.

On other occasions, the learner's needs may be more complicated than simply needing to practise or revise more thoroughly. Difficulties or problems in their lives may be having an impact on their educational progress. Coping with the consequences of an accident or a family bereavement may not leave much time, opportunity or energy to devote to completing assignments. At times like this, institutions and awarding bodies have procedures in place to help. Sometimes, allowing learners some extra time may be all that is required. At other times, the learner may have to leave the course that they are on and rejoin later. Any teacher or trainer in any educational setting may encounter situations such as these – even someone who is only recently qualified. At times like this, it is important to follow the correct procedures as laid out by the awarding body. Appropriate guidelines will appear in the course handbooks and regulations that are sent out to education and training providers. For a new tutor, speaking to a more experienced colleague, or to a mentor, may be more appropriate.

On other occasions, assessment can highlight a more profound need. This may be related to a lack of previous formal achievement in education such as poor numeracy or literacy skills: these issues are covered in Chapter 2. In addition, assessment may highlight a learning disability or difficulty that has not been diagnosed before: this issue is discussed in Chapter 9.

3. Providing public acknowledgement and certification of learning

Receiving official notice of success at the end of a course is undeniably an exciting moment, making all the time spent preparing and practising seem worthwhile. Sometimes, a slip of paper giving examination results is all that is received. At other times, learners receive certificates: sometimes by post, sometimes handed out at a public ceremony. The receipt of a certificate is public proof that the learner has met the required standards, as laid down by the awarding body, for the area or subject in which the qualification has been awarded.

4. Allowing processes of selection to be carried out

So what do the learners actually do with their certificates? For some, the receipt of one qualification or set of qualifications acts as a stepping-stone to another programme of study. For example, the successful completion of an access course will allow the learner to move on to higher education; or the award of an NVQ at level 2 will allow the learner to progress to level 3. On other occasions, the qualification will allow the learner entry to an area of work: for example, a learner who has completed qualifications in hair and beauty to the required level can then seek employment in the hair and beauty industry. Future employers will not necessarily look for potential employees with specific qualifications; rather, they will judge a candidate's suitability and potential based on their previous achievement as a whole. A candidate with qualifications in one particular area or discipline may show the potential to make a success of a job in a different sphere. There are many people who have an interest in the results of assessment, not just tutors and learners. This issue is discussed in more detail in Chapter 8.

5. Providing a way to evaluate learning programmes

Clearly, the main aim of assessment is to find out how much learning has taken place. But what if there was something wrong with the way that the course was organised or delivered? Mistakes do happen, and awarding bodies, colleges and tutors are not perfect. By carefully scrutinising the results of the assessment process, it is possible to identify those aspects of the programme that may need further development. This issue is discussed in more detail in Chapter 8.

6. Motivating and encouraging learners

Exploring the reasons why people participate in post-compulsory education is not straightforward. A lot of research has been done on this topic, and the results tend to be discussed in terms of categories of motivation. For example, one learner may be studying for a qualification because without it, he may lose his job or fail to gain promotion, or a pay rise, in his current post. Another may be studying for the same qualification purely out of interest in the subject being studied: for her, it is a simple personal choice. A third may be attending because, having left school with no formal qualifications, he feels embarrassed or ashamed by his previous failure, and is seeking to keep up with friends and family. A fourth may be studying because she is seeking to go on to higher study, and this course is a necessary prerequisite. As teachers and trainers in the Lifelong Learning sector, we will at times encounter a bewildering variety of learners, and many of them will have very different reasons for wanting to take part.

Assessment will always be more problematic for some learners than others, even those who have chosen to return to education. The role of the teacher or trainer is, therefore, partly to motivate those learners: to help build up their confidence so that they can tackle the portfolios, tests and examinations that they will encounter. And the feedback that the learners receive can also help to motivate them further, through offering praise and recognition of work done well, in addition to providing guidance on what needs to be done next.

When do we assess?

Timing is another characteristic of the assessment process that has changed during recent years. There has been a significant shift away from assessment being carried out mainly at the end of a programme of study, towards a more continuous pattern of assessment where the learner's progress is tested throughout the course. These issues will be discussed in more detail in Chapter 3.

Over recent years, the importance of pre-programme assessment – diagnostic assessment – has become well established. It is discussed in detail in Chapter 2.

Who is involved in assessment?

As teachers and trainers, we are at the front line of assessment: we are the ones who work in classrooms, lecture halls, workshops and laboratories. We explain to the learners what they have to do, sometimes designing the assessment tasks ourselves. We mark assignments and give feedback, and we record those marks using appropriate forms and documents (an issue discussed in detail in Chapter 7). If one of our learners has a problem (and these problems can come in many forms), then it is the teacher who will be the first port of call for advice or help. But we do not work in isolation. The assignments and examinations that we help our learners to succeed in are to be found in many institutional contexts in different parts of the country. Some qualifications operate on a regional level, others on a national scale: the number of learners all working towards the same assignment at any one time can run into thousands. There are many regional and national organisations in place that work to sustain the qualifications framework of the further education sector. So who is involved in assessment?

The tutor

The responsibilities of the tutor will vary according to a number of factors: the subject area in which she works; her experience or seniority; the number of learners that she is responsible for and the way in which roles and responsibilities are organised within her place of work. As well as setting and marking assignments, tutors may, over time, take on additional responsibilities, such as second marking or internal moderation (discussed in Chapter 8) or course leadership roles, which may involve direct liaison with awarding bodies.

The learner

As teachers and trainers, our first responsibility is to our learners: they are the reason why we do the jobs that we do. The relationship between tutors and learners has changed quite drastically over the last century, informed by both changing social attitudes as well as changing understanding of the education and training process. And assessment has changed as well. Over the last two decades, we have seen a decisive shift away from assessment that is broadly examination based and concentrated at the end of a programme of study, towards assessment that is continuous and that can be carried out using a variety of methods. Learners are encouraged to think about how and why they are assessed, and in some cases, learners can even influence the ways in which they are assessed. It is no longer the case that assessment is simply something that is done to the learner. Rather, learners are encouraged to take ownership of the process.

The place of study

Much, though by no means all, assessment practice is carried out at the place of study. It might be a college or adult education centre, providing learners with the resources needed for their programme of study: learning resource centres containing books, computers, magazines and CD-ROMs; workshops; kitchens; salons and classrooms. Many colleges work in their local community and with local employers to provide a range of education and training services. They often collaborate with community education providers or local authorities to offer courses of study in a range of settings such as specially designated classrooms in primary or secondary schools or local libraries. Not all adult education practitioners are so fortunate in terms of the resources that are available to them, however. For those who deliver part-time evening classes in a community setting (and it could be a church hall or a function room above a pub) any resources that are required for assessment may need to be created and carried about by the tutors themselves.

The awarding body

An awarding body is an organisation that operates on a regional or national basis and offers formal qualifications. The awarding body is ultimately responsible for setting out the work required for the qualification to be awarded (the curriculum), for ensuring that providers are offering awards to the required standard (a process known as validation) and for making sure that across the many colleges offering awards, assessment and marking are fair (a process known as moderation). These issues will be discussed in depth in Chapter 8.

For a new tutor, the list of different awarding bodies can seem baffling, especially because they are invariably referred to by their initials. For example: City and Guilds (C&G) or the Business and Technology Education Council (BTEC). Some awarding bodies have now dropped their full title altogether. The body once called the Northern Council for Further

Education is now known simply as NCFE. In addition, a number of professional bodies are also involved in the accreditation of qualifications, such as the Chartered Institute of Personnel Development (CIPD) or the Association of Accountancy Technicians (AAT).

Government

Education policy accounts for a considerable amount of work done, and public money spent, by the government, through the Department for Education (DfE). For many writers and commentators, the thinking that supports much current education policy dates back to 1976, when the then Prime Minister James Callaghan made a speech that stressed the importance of education in preparing people for work. He also called for education to be more accountable to parents and employers. Many of the changes brought about by governments since this time can be interpreted in the light of these ideas. The thinking of successive governments has been influenced by independent research, lobbying from parents, employers and businesses and changing national and international economic trends.

In October 2004, the Working Group on 14-19 Reform published a report called *14-19 Curriculum and Qualifications Reform*. This report, which is referred to as the Tomlinson Report (Mike Tomlinson is the chair of the Working Group), called for a thorough overhaul of the assessment and qualifications regime that is currently in place for 14 to 19 year olds, arguing (among other things) that it is necessary to establish a greater parity between vocational and academic qualifications, and to reduce both the burden of assessment on learners, teachers and institutions (which is currently too great) and the number of qualifications and specifications that are currently in place (of which there are too many, creating confusion). In place of the current assessment and curriculum system would come a new diploma that would see a reduction in external assessment (that is to say, assessment that is designed, moderated and administered by regional or national bodies that are outside colleges) and an extension of the role of teacher assessment in its place. The report also calls for a streamlining of the paperwork and record keeping that current assessment systems require. The government's response was mixed. After considering the Tomlinson report, the government decided to leave the academic curriculum (A levels and GCSEs) untouched, and to focus reform on the technical and vocational curricula instead.

This is not the first time that changes within education and training have led to changes in assessment practice. Earlier examples include the introduction of General National Vocational Qualifications (GNVQs) in 1992, and the introduction of AS levels in 2000. While changes in assessment practice are readily experienced in our working lives, changing ideas and theories relating to assessment (often bound up in theory and research relating to learning and teaching more generally) tend not to have such an immediate impact.

In 2006, the Department for Education and Skills published *Further Education: Raising Skills, Improving Life Chances*, which set out an ambitious programme for reform of the learning and skills sector, including a new, simpler vocational qualifications framework based around a specialised diploma for 14-19 learners. These 14-19 Diplomas, which were first rolled out in 2008, consist of three elements. Firstly, there is the **principal learning** element (which relates to the specific occupational area that the Diploma rests in). Secondly, there is the **generic learning** element (which includes functional skills, which we shall return to in Chapter 2). And finally, there is the **additional learning** element (which consists of optional components that allow an element of personalisation for each learner). However, the take-up of Diplomas has been significantly lower than anticipated. Together with the anticipated (at the time of writing this) changes to assessment and learning more generally that have been signalled by the publication of Professor Alison Wolf's review into vocational and technical education, it would appear that 14-19 qualifications are once again to be 'reformed'.

And overall . . .

While it is tempting to concentrate our attention on the immediate context in which we teach or train, an awareness of the broader trends and ideas that have an impact on education and training as a whole, and on assessment in particular, can be both valuable and useful. As new teachers and trainers, our primary concerns will be focused almost exclusively on those assessment activities and procedures that are of immediate importance: setting class-based tests, marking assignments and providing guidance to our learners when compiling portfolios, for example. However, it will not take long for the influence of some of these other interested parties to make itself felt: it is not uncommon for an awarding body to change the specifications of a qualification, and hence the assessment needed to achieve it, only a year after the previous specifications have been published. Changes to the way in which colleges receive funding can lead to an expansion of particular types of course, sometimes at the expense of other areas of the curriculum. And as we grow and develop as professionals, many tutors will take on additional responsibilities that necessitate regular contact with external bodies. It is important, therefore, sometimes to look at the bigger picture, as well as concentrating on the detail of our own teaching practice.

A SUMMARY OF **KEY POINTS**

In this chapter, we have looked at the following key themes:

> **definitions of assessment;**
> **the reasons why assessment is important;**
> **the stakeholders in the assessment process.**

It may seem odd to question fundamental issues such as why we assess and why it is important, when much of our lives as teachers and trainers will be spent dealing with matters relating to assessment. As you read this book, questioning these issues may help you articulate your own beliefs or philosophies about what is important in education and training. The questions may only be tangential to this book, but they are directly relevant to the exploration of professional values and ethics that underpin teacher training as a whole.

REFERENCES AND FURTHER READING

Armitage, A, Bryant, R, Dunnill, R, Renwick, M, Hayes, D, Hudson, A, Kent, J and Lawes, S (2007) *Teaching and Training in Post-Compulsory Education* Third edition. Maidenhead: Open University Press. Chapter 9 contains a valuable and thorough chronology of events and changes relating to post-compulsory education and training.

Lea, J, Hayes, D, Armitage, A, Lomas, L and Markless, S (2003) *Working in Post-Compulsory Education*. Maidenhead: Open University Press. Chapter 1 contains a valuable summary of political ideas relating to post-compulsory education over the last 25 years.

The official press release relating to the Wolf review of vocational education is at: www.education. gov.uk/inthenews/pressnotices/a0075181/wolf-review-proposes-major-reform-of-vocational-education

2
Diagnostic assessment, AP(E)L and ipsative assessment

By the end of this chapter you should:

- **understand a variety of reasons why diagnostic assessment is carried out;**
- **know how the results of diagnostic assessment can be used to help plan for learning;**
- **understand ways in which prior experience can be accredited as learning;**
- **know how diagnostic assessment can be used to diagnose specific learner needs.**

Professional Standards

This chapter relates to the following Professional Standards.

Professional Values

ES1: Designing and using assessment as a tool for learning and progression.

Professional Knowledge and Understanding

EK1.1: Theories and principles of assessment, and the application of different forms of assessment, including initial, formative and summative assessment, in teaching and learning.

Professional Practice

EP1.1: Use appropriate forms of assessment and evaluate their effectiveness in producing information useful to the teacher and the learner.

PRACTICAL TASK PRACTICAL TASK PRACTICAL TASK PRACTICAL TASK PRACTICAL TASK

Learners often undergo assessment before and at the very start of a programme of study. Talk to your mentor, or if you do not have a mentor, try to speak to an experienced tutor who works in the same subject area as you do. Think about the ways in which learners are assessed before or at the very beginning of a particular course or programme of study, and write them down. Go through the list and evaluate each point: think about exactly what is being assessed. Is it particular skills or competences, such as use of number or IT skills? Or is the learner being assessed in more subject-specific terms, perhaps to decide whether he or she is suitable for entry onto that course in particular?

What is diagnostic assessment?

At the start of the academic year, or at the start of any new course or programme of study, teachers and trainers will get to meet their new group or groups of learners. Some of us will be meeting them for the first time, while others may have met some or all of the learners before, during interviews or open days. Some learners will be returning to start a new course after successfully achieving a qualification last year. Others will be returning to study after a period of paid employment or after raising a family. Before starting the course, many learners will have gone through an official admission process, to judge their suitability for the course in question. On many adult education courses, however, application processes may be significantly less formal: many still run an 'open-door' policy to recruitment, with the effect that diagnostic assessment, whether formal or informal, becomes, in the first instance, the sole responsibility of the tutor. Nonetheless, formal application procedures are becoming more widespread. This may have consisted of an interview, or an application form, or both, and this process of selection is in itself a form of initial diagnostic assessment: assessment that identifies the characteristics, competencies, skills or knowledge of the learner. It allows teachers and trainers to guide the learner towards their goals, identifying what those goals should be, and what we need to do to help the learner achieve them.

It is not only at the early stages of a learner's career that practitioners need to diagnose learning needs, however: continuing diagnostic assessment will in fact occur at several stages of the learning process.

Diagnostic assessment before a course:

- **provides initial guidance and advice;**
- **identifies entry criteria for the programme together with any possible claim for accreditation of prior learning.**

Diagnostic assessment before and during a course:

- **reviews learner progress through progress review or tutorial meetings;**
- **identifies learner's strengths and development needs;**
- **identifies learning strategies and activities that the learner uses or may need to develop.**

Diagnostic assessment before the course

The first occasion when we need to use initial diagnostic assessment is in giving advice to our prospective learners before the course begins. The tutor's role here is to help point the learner in the right direction, matching the learner to the most suitable programme and giving advice and guidance about the courses available to meet the learner's needs. This is not a matter for the tutor to decide in isolation, of course: awarding bodies very often set specific entry requirements for certain courses. These may be described as prerequisites or pre-entry conditions within a course manual or handbook. On these occasions, the process of assessment is used simply to determine whether the learner has already reached the level of study and/or competence required for entry to the course. Entry to a programme of study may be dependent on the learner having already obtained certain qualifications, or having comparable relevant experience. For work-based learning programmes or vocational training programmes, appropriate workplace experience may be a prerequisite of commencing study. Work placements may be a necessary component of the programme itself.

In this example, the pre-entry conditions are quite straightforward, and relate simply to prior qualifications or experience:

Some learners may begin working towards this HSC Diploma after achieving units from 'entry to the sector' or 'induction' qualifications. A close correlation will exist between these entry/induction units and the mandatory units in the Diploma, i.e. they will share the same knowledge content.

Level 2 Diploma in Health and Social Care

In this next example, however, the entry requirements are a little more complicated. The learner has to have already achieved certain qualifications and to have access to sufficient relevant work experience:

Candidates **must** be qualified to level 3, or be able to demonstrate level 3 process skills and personal skills in the subject they intend to teach, have access to **150** teaching practice hours and possess reasonable levels in areas of language, literacy, numeracy and ICT not represented within their subject specialism.

Potential trainees must be able to:

- demonstrate the ability to use the functional processes of mathematics whilst engaging with contexts that require extended mathematical problem solving to be resolved;
- think in extended logic chains involving multiple steps. This should occur both within processing and analysis elements and holistically across all elements of the functional process;
- demonstrate good understanding when working in familiar situations; this will enable demonstration of secure processing skills (the ability to use and apply mathematics in a context is often governed, amongst other things by the degree of familiarity);
- demonstrate development of understanding by investigation in unfamiliar situations; this will support demonstration of mathematical transferability and development of mathematical conceptualisation.

Level 5 Diploma in Teaching Mathematics (Numeracy) in the
Lifelong Learning sector

Many programmes of study, however, do not have such specific requirements:

There are no entry qualifications or age limits required for these qualifications unless this is a legal requirement of the process or the environment. Assessment is open to any candidate who has the potential to reach the standards laid down for this qualification.

Scheme handbook 1681 for Level 3 City and Guilds NVQ in Fabrication and
Welding Engineering

In our first two examples, the criteria laid down by the awarding body provided the guidelines for the admissions process. Candidates with appropriate prior qualifications can be easily matched to appropriate courses in situations such as these. In the third example, the tutor is being asked to make a judgement about the learner's potential, and in these situations, the tutor will make use of the college's own admissions procedures, which have been designed to assess the candidate's suitability for the course in question, and may consist of any or all of the following components:

- a personal statement made by the candidate on an application form or CV;
- a reference from a previous tutor or employer, setting out the candidate's suitability for the course;
- previous educational experience and/or qualifications and other records of achievement in other areas;
- an interview;
- a prerequisite test or entrance examination.

REFLECTIVE TASK

Spend a few minutes considering the entry requirements for your teacher-training course. Write down all the forms of initial diagnostic assessment that you experienced (interview, pre-enrolment written tests, application forms etc.) How do you think that this information is used, when it is gathered together? Do you think that it influences the way your teacher-training course is delivered?

Accreditation of prior (experiential) learning (APEL)

APEL recognises learning that has resulted from prior work and life experience, and allows colleges to recognise and give credit for it. This makes APEL an important part of the drive to widen access to education for people who have been under-represented in education (particular social or ethnic groups) or to make it easier for people with no formal qualifications to re-enter education. It opens up all kinds of education, training and accreditation opportunities for people who lack formal qualifications and certificates but can still prove that 'they can do it' – that they have achieved a particular skill, competence or understanding. Diverse learning from experience is just as important as the learning that takes place in schools and colleges, and APEL provides a way for it to be recognised and rewarded, motivating people to re-enter formal education when they might otherwise have been excluded.

APEL can be based on different types or sources of evidence:

- evidence of achievement in the workplace, such as letters of commendation or documents demonstrating workplace responsibilities;
- documents or objects/materials demonstrating achievement in the workplace, possibly created by the learner at work;
- references or testimonials written by employers, clients or customers;
- evidence of community or voluntary activities.

As well as allowing entry to a programme, an APEL claim can be used to gain exemption from individual parts of a programme. If the candidate's prior experience can be shown to be equivalent to parts of the course, it can be officially recognised or accredited. The candidate has to compile an APEL claim, putting together evidence that he or she has already met the learning outcomes for the unit through prior experiential learning, and avoiding having to study for a module or unit that he or she 'can already do'.

A note on terminology

APEL and APL are often used interchangeably, but they are not the same thing. APL – the accreditation of prior learning – refers to prior learning that has been accredited and where a certificate, or other formal record of achievement, has been awarded on successful completion.

APL is a little different from APEL, therefore, as it emphasises prior qualifications. The accreditation of prior learning allows a candidate to start a course or programme of study when her/his qualifications are not the standard entry qualifications required by the course. APL can be used by the candidate to claim exemption from specific units or modules if by achieving a prior qualification, the candidate has already met the learning outcomes of specific units in the new course or programme of study.

THEORY FOCUS **THEORY** FOCUS **THEORY** FOCUS **THEORY** FOCUS **THEORY** FOCUS

'The fundamental principle underpinning APEL is that learning is worthy and capable of gaining recognition and credit, regardless of the time, place and context in which it has been achieved. It thus represents a move to accept that learning is not dependent upon any particular formal setting, and to acknowledge it as being of value in its own right.'

Challis (1993) page 1

Within APEL the distinction is frequently made between formal and informal learning. Put simply, formal learning is learning that takes place in a formal setting or institution: a college or a community education centre, for example. Informal learning is learning that takes place in our daily lives: in the workplace, in the home or in our community. APEL provides a method by which this informal learning, which is difficult to quantify and also difficult to assign a value to, can be recognised as being worthwhile and valuable.

APEL/APL evidence checklist

Any materials that a learner wishes to use to make an APEL or APL claim will need to meet the following requirements:

- **Is it *valid*? Does the evidence match the learning outcomes of the course that the candidate wishes to join or claim exemption from?**
- **Is it *reliable*? Will two different tutors both agree that the evidence meets course requirements?**
- **Is it *sufficient*? Is there enough evidence to cover all aspects of the course?**
- **Is it *authentic*? Is the evidence the property of the candidate?**
- **Is it *current*? Is the evidence up-to-date? Normally, five years is considered as a 'cut-off point' for evidence in APEL/APL claims.**

NOTE
These concepts are important for all forms of assessment and not just APEL/APL. They will be explored in detail in Chapter 4. If necessary, refer to Chapter 4 and then return here.

Summary: APEL/APL

The APEL/APL process can be summed up as follows:

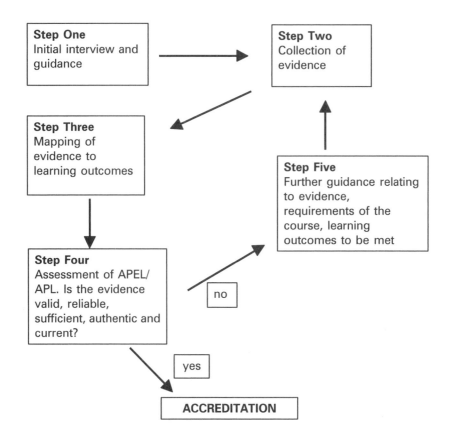

Learners with particular requirements

As well as helping make a decision about which options are best for the prospective learner, the process of diagnostic assessment can also reveal any specific support needs that the learner may have. A learner who is deaf or partially-hearing, for example, may need particular technical equipment, or a note-taker to help them during their studies. They may need access to rooms where an induction loop has been installed. In situations such as this, specialist assessments are often necessary. As teachers and trainers we may not be qualified to carry out such assessments ourselves, but we do need to know where we can find appropriate support in our institution. The results of this specialist diagnostic assessment will have to be circulated to a number of people. If there is one, then the Learning Support office may need to be involved if a learning support assistant is needed. The estates office will have to be informed if technical equipment needs to be installed. For part-time tutors, especially those working away from large institutions, such situations pose particular challenges, as specialist equipment and advice can be hard to locate. Part-time tutors working on behalf of large organisations such as local education authorities, or the Workers Educational Association, are not always made sufficiently aware of the resources available to them. Self-employed tutors, on the other hand, may need to invest in appropriate resources themselves. And, of course, the teacher or trainer of the course in question needs to be informed, so that lessons, activities, assessments and resources can be planned appropriately.

These issues, and their implications, are discussed in detail in Chapter 9.

Diagnostic assessment during the course

Tutorial support

The kinds of assessment that teachers and trainers have to carry out and evaluate vary according to their role. Not all teachers and trainers have formal responsibilities for admissions to a programme of study, for example. And some have responsibilities beyond simply delivering modules or units. As well as being class tutors, we may be given roles as personal tutors or progress tutors, staying with a learner throughout their time at college. The learner may be taught by several members of staff during a programme, but the progress or personal tutor acts as a permanent source of advice and guidance. Regularly reviewing a learner's progress will help identify any further support needs, should difficulties come to light during the programme, and give the learner the opportunity to raise any concerns or questions that he or she might have. Reports from meetings such as this, often recorded in a progress file or individual learning plan, complement assessments carried out during the modules or units that the learner is studying, and help to provide a picture of overall progress and achievement. A number of ways of recording and disseminating such information will be explored in Chapter 7.

Specific aptitude assessments: functional skills

Since the publication of the Moser Report, *A Fresh Start: Improving Literacy and Numeracy*, the development of literacy and numeracy skills has been a central, and much debated, component of provision within the learning and skills sector. Courses for younger learners at colleges, for work-based learners, and for adults attending classes in community settings have benefited from new core curricula, new sources of funding and newly qualified staff. And yet the nature of this provision continues to change and be changed: it would seem that barely a year goes by without a new literacy or numeracy initiative being launched by the appropriate government department or agency (which themselves change name and focus with sometimes bewildering speed). Over the last ten years we have moved from 'core skills' towards 'basic skills', through to 'key skills' and now to 'functional skills'. As teachers and trainers in the Lifelong Learning sector, we now find ourselves delivering functional skills which might be embedded within a GCSE or Diploma, or might be a stand-alone qualification. But what are functional skills? The Qualifications and Curriculum Authority (QCA) defines them as follows:

> *Functional skills are practical skills in English, Information and Communication Technology (ICT) and Mathematics, that allow individuals to work confidently, effectively and independently in life.*

The diverse nature of the learner population in the Lifelong Learning sector is reflected in the wide range of prior experiences and qualifications that are found amongst them. Many learners come to college already in possession of 'good' passes in English and/or mathematics at GCSE. Many others do not, however, and for these learners, a functional skills curriculum may provide an appropriate alternative to gaining the skills that they will need in English, mathematics and ICT. For this reason, many colleges ask new learners to undergo diagnostic assessment in numeracy and literacy (and sometimes ICT as well) in order to ascertain future learning needs. This process may also contribute to the diagnosis of specific learning difficulties. On adult education programmes, by contrast, functional skills support does not form part of the formal curriculum.

Teacher-education programmes in post-16 education are also catching up with these requirements. FENTO (the predecessor to LLUK) introduced language, literacy and numeracy requirements for teachers and trainers in further education, and this 'minimum core' was incorporated into the PCET teacher-education curriculum in September 2004, although the ways in which they are assessed across the teacher-training curriculum are rather divergent. Many providers of teacher training for the Lifelong Learning sector do assess the literacy and numeracy skills of their trainee teachers. However, having literacy and numeracy qualifications at level 2 is not a requirement of the PGCE/CertEd/DTLLS syllabus. Rather, it is only during *professional formation* in order to achieve QTLS that they are required.

The following extract comes from a learning journal kept by David, who is a lecturer in carpentry. He taught on a casual basis for two terms and has now moved to a full-time post after many years working in the construction industry. He has recently begun studying for his teaching qualification on a part-time basis.

> Third week of the course. Our tutor explained that we all had to do literacy and numeracy tests as part of our teacher training. Anyway, off we went and we did the tests on computers in the learning resource centre. I didn't mind this too much because I have a PC at home, but Ann was much more nervous as she hardly uses computers.
>
> I never worried about maths because I was quite good at maths at school but my English was never really good. In the end though I got the same scores for both. It's quite funny really – at first I was really nervous because I hadn't done an exam for absolutely ages but in the end it was all right.

REFLECTIVE TASK

Does the teacher-training course that you are currently enrolled on include numeracy and literacy testing? If the answer is 'yes', spend a few minutes answering these questions: How did it feel when you took the tests? Were the results as you expected? Were they done on computers, or were they written tests? Which format (on screen or paper-based) do you prefer, and why? Did you share your results with anyone?

David's learning journal raises important issues relating to assessment in general, not just the assessment of literacy or numeracy skills. Some learners are nervous about assessment and this could have an impact on how well they perform when being tested. And learners often draw on the memories of previous educational experience. These are personal, emotional issues that teachers and trainers always need to be aware of.

The decision to test David and the rest of his group using computers raises a different kind of issue, however, relating to choice of assessment methods. David referred to a fellow learner, Ann, who was not as comfortable with the on-screen assessment as he was. Should Ann have been allowed to sit a paper-based literacy and numeracy test rather than an on-screen test? If so, would she have received a different result? It may be true that Ann needs to develop her IT skills, but it seems unfair that the diagnosis of her current numeracy and literacy levels should be affected by her having to carry out an assessment using a method with which she is unfamiliar. Perhaps Ann's and David's teacher should have asked whether any of the group would have preferred an alternative format for the test. But then how could their teacher be sure of receiving consistent results for the group as a whole? Issues of consistency will be returned to in Chapters 4 and 8, and issues relating to the provision of alternative forms of assessment in the light of individual needs will be explored in Chapter 9.

Literacy and numeracy assessment such as this is not simply a functional process: the aim of the minimum core is not just to check up on the literacy and numeracy levels of trainee lecturers. There are broader issues that will affect our teaching and training. First, the impact of social and cultural factors on numeracy and literacy development (such as the challenges faced by learners for whom English is not a first language); second, the impact of learning difficulties and disabilities on numeracy and literacy acquisition (such as the challenges faced by blind or partially-sighted learners who may need to have learning materials redesigned). Chapter 9 considers issues of access to assessment in more detail.

Specific aptitude assessments: preferred styles of learning

At the start of each new academic year, I ask all the learners on my teacher-education course to note down, briefly, an answer to the question 'When and where do you do your best private study?' Here are some of the answers I have received

- **Early in the morning, at a desk or in the library. By lunchtime, I lose my concentration.**
- **During the day, really – at night, I cannot get down to work at all.**
- **It does not really matter, but I do like to have a room to work in that is really well-lit, and I like the radio to be on.**
- **On the sofa, with all my books and notes scattered all over the floor.**

Following this, I then go on to ask 'How do you do your best private study?' The responses to this question are very different:

- **Reading and taking notes as I go. Then I read the notes back to myself afterwards.**
- **I find that sometimes I talk out loud to myself when I write assignments.**
- **I like to photocopy chapters from books and then I go over them with a highlighter and mark the important bits when reading.**
- **I do not like working on my own as much as working with the others. I like the classes when you can talk and share ideas.**

These are answers that we can all empathise with, even if we do not share these particular experiences. And they highlight an issue that is 'common sense' to some people, whereas for others it is the cornerstone of a 'learner-centred approach' – the different ways in which people learn. Arguments and theories about how people learn are many and varied. Educational researchers, psychologists, scientists, training consultants – all these groups and more have had an input into debates about learning and teaching. Many of these areas of research are outside the scope of this book, but the argument about how people learn is of relevance, and not just because it is included in the LLUK standards. An understanding of the different ways in which people learn is a vital component of the learning and teaching process and helps teachers and trainers to design and plan lessons in ways which will generate interest and understanding in all our learners.

In this extract from her learning journal, Julie, a new lecturer in childcare studies, writes about her experiences in giving a learning styles assessment to her new level 2 group:

> I decided to set aside the first half of the session for learning styles after talking to my mentor – she did this last year and it took her a bit over an hour. I started off by explaining to the group why they had to complete the questionnaire and I told them that the results would help me when planning classes. I also told them that they should not just do the test and forget about it, but think about what the tests told them about how they learn best. The test itself went okay and was quite quick although a couple of the questions seemed a bit stupid and then they all counted up their scores and we went round the class and everyone said what kind of learner they were (Visual, Auditory, or Kinaesthetic). Two of the girls had two scores that were the same and I hoped that it would make the discussion more interesting because I thought that they had all assumed that they would just have one learning style.
>
> I'm not sure it worked all that well, though and I do not think they all took it seriously. Jackie said that if she was a visual learner then all she wanted to do each week was watch videos, and then Nicky said that as she was a kinaesthetic learner, did that mean that she didn't have to read the textbook? And I wasn't too sure if they were being serious, or just being silly. So in the end it did take the whole of the first part of the session because I had to get through to them all that they shouldn't just be learning according to their highest score, but practise learning in the other ways too.

Julie decided that she should tell her group exactly why she was asking them to complete the learning styles assessment. Offering explanations like this is considered good practice in all forms of assessment: explaining how and why assessment happens helps learners to engage with the process of assessment and to get the most out of it (as we saw in Chapter 1). In this case, the learning styles assessment process also contributed to the learners' Key Skills development, specifically *improving own learning and performance*. By understanding how they learn best, Julie's learners can acquire and/or practise using those strategies that meet their needs best. During tutorials or progress review meetings, the learners can discuss their relevant Key Skills development with their tutor and ask for advice relating to their learning style. Julie can also take care to include appropriate learning and teaching strategies in her lessons to meet the varied learning styles of her group.

So far so good, but Julie has asked for more than this: she wants her learners to *practise learning in other ways too*. Her approach to learning styles includes a wish to see her learners work to develop those approaches that at the moment, according to the diagnostic assessment, they do not favour. In this piece of reflective writing, Julie explains her perspective:

> Different parts of the course need to be taught in different ways – I'm sure of it. I can see how some of the group may not like doing a lot of reading, whether it's from the set text or from handouts or something else, and would prefer to do more hands-on things instead. But I cannot teach the underpinning knowledge as a practical! At some point, they have to take some notes and learn facts and information and things! Surely the different parts of the course need to be taught in different ways? The important thing is for me to plan lots of activities that are really varied, so that all the different learning styles get something out of each session. But I think that I need to make them learn in all the other ways as well as the way in which they got their highest scores.

Julie has highlighted two important areas of debate here: first, to what extent does what she is teaching influence how she needs to teach it? This is important because this question leads to us asking: to what extent does what she is teaching influence how she needs to assess it? We will return to this in Chapter 5. Second, to what extent should she encourage her learners to develop across all learning styles, rather than just stick with what, according to the diagnostic assessment, is their preferred style?

THEORY FOCUS **THEORY** FOCUS **THEORY** FOCUS **THEORY** FOCUS **THEORY** FOCUS

In their research on using learning styles, Frank Coffield, David Moseley, Elaine Hall and Kathryn Ecclestone examined 13 different learning styles models and their uses in post-16 education. Amongst other things, they said:

'... pressures on colleges to meet inspection criteria for ... diagnostic assessment during student induction may lead to an unthinking and uncritical administration of a learning style inventory ...'

Coffield et al (2004) page 10

We shall explore the impact of inspection on assessment in Chapter 8. But the message is clear: if, as teachers and trainers, we simply ask our learners to spend time completing learning styles assessments only to file the results away in our progress files without really doing much with them, then it is not really worth doing at all! In the example above, Julie has touched on two other key issues raised by Coffield et al. Firstly, they argue that different ways of knowing and understanding need different ways of learning and teaching; secondly, they point out that of the 13 learning styles models that they explored, only one explicitly acknowledges the importance for learners to develop across different learning styles rather than just use their preferred styles. Nor are practitioners such as Julie helped by the fact that there are so many different learning styles models to choose from.

In practice the choice of which learning styles questionnaire to use is dictated by college departmental policy rather than the individual, in much the same way that the choice of assessment methods, especially summative assessment, is generally made for teachers or trainers rather than by them. However, if as practitioners we can avoid using learning styles to categorise or stereotype our learners, but use them carefully and critically to engage our learners and ourselves with the learning process, then this form of diagnostic assessment can help us help our learners to learn.

Ipsative assessment

Encouraging learners to reflect on ways to facilitate and improve their learning, and seek them out, is a process involving the learner and the tutor in dialogue facilitated by feedback. The teacher or trainer is responsible for any or all of the following:

- **applying and managing the diagnostic assessments;**
- **collecting and interpreting the results;**
- **acting on these results in the classroom or workshop;**
- **working with the learner through tutorials or progress review meetings by acting on these results and using them to facilitate the learner's progress.**

The feedback processes that characterise the dialogue between the tutor and the learner will be discussed in detail in Chapter 6.

If we are to help learners improve their own learning and performance, however, we need to encourage them to think about their own progress, to consider for themselves how they think they are doing and to become responsible for thinking about their own approach to learning. We need to encourage our learners to assess themselves on an individual basis (assessing each other – peer assessment – will be considered in Chapter 3). This form of self-assessment is also referred to as ipsative assessment.

What is ipsative assessment?

As a diagnostic process, ipsative assessment can be defined as an individual process of self-assessment that allows the learner to:

- **identify their own initial strengths and weaknesses (entry behaviours);**
- **set self-defined targets against which future progress will be assessed;**
- **assess their needs independently of their teacher or trainer.**

For this process to be a meaningful one for the learner, they will need a very clear under-standing of the direction or purpose of the learning programme that is being undertaken. It is a way of encouraging learner autonomy (as discussed in Chapter 1), and developing the learner's confidence as well as helping the learner acquire functional skills.

Ipsative assessment or self-assessment can also be used during a programme of study, as learners reflect on their progress in relation to the targets that were agreed at the diagnosis stage described above. I will return to this in Chapter 3.

BEELECLIAE 1V2K

REFLECTIVE TASK

Reflective practice has a significant and widespread role within the curriculum for post-16 teacher education. Many courses ask trainee lecturers to engage in reflective practice as a form of self-assessment, for example by using learning journals. If as practitioners in the Lifelong Learning sector we are constantly reflecting on what and how we learn and how we apply that learning, why should we not encourage similar reflective practice amongst our learners?

Spend a few minutes thinking about and writing down the key ideas, uses and issues surrounding reflective practice. Then, for each of these, consider ways in which they could apply to one particular group or cohort of learners whom you teach or train.

A SUMMARY OF **KEY POINTS**

In this chapter, we have looked at the following key themes:
- > **diagnostic assessment to help learners gain access to appropriate education and training opportunities;**
- > **diagnostic assessment to help identify specific learners' needs, particularly relating to functional skills and individual learner styles;**
- > **the potential uses for ipsative assessment processes during the diagnostic stage.**

Although the principles that underpin diagnostic assessments are important and compelling, the teacher and trainer need to pay careful attention to follow up or act on the results of such assessments if they are not to turn into another exercise in form-filling. We must also be prepared to help learners return to the issues, needs and targets highlighted by the diagnostic assessment process throughout their time on the course.

Branching options

Reflection

How is diagnostic assessment implemented in your professional practice? Do you teach on non-accredited adult education courses that have an open door policy, and would you welcome a more formal admissions process? Or do you teach on vocational courses with strict entry criteria, and are these rigidly adhered to?

Analysis

Ipsative assessment can be a powerful tool to aid motivation and increase learner engagement. Take one group of learners with whom you are currently working. Is there space for ipsative assessment strategies within the programme? Or are they all working to the same imposed standards?

Research

APEL is still a feature of the teacher training programme that I teach. But how common is it in the Lifelong Learning sector as a whole? There used to be specialist qualifications in giving learners APEL advice, but these seem less common. As you research APEL in more depth, focus on APEL as part of a broader widening participation strategy, and research programmes of study where APEL is still practised.

REFERENCES AND FURTHER READING

Butterworth, C (1992) More than one bite at the APEL – contrasting models of accrediting prior learning. *Journal of Further and Higher Education* 16(3) pp39-51.

Challis, M (1993) *Introducing APEL.* London: Routledge.

Coffield, F, Moseley, D, Hall, E and Ecclestone, K (2004) *Should We Be Using Learning Styles? What research has to say to practice.* Trowbridge: Learning and Skills Research Centre.

Scott, I (2010) But I know that already: rhetoric or reality – the accreditation of prior experiential learning in the context of work-based learning. *Research in Post-Compulsory Education* 15(1) pp19-31.

3
Formative and summative assessment

PRACTICAL TASK PRACTICAL TASK PRACTICAL TASK PRACTICAL TASK PRACTICAL TASK

Before reading on, spend a few minutes thinking about the ways in which your learners are assessed during and at the end of one particular course or unit for which you are the teacher or trainer. Write them down in a list, and next to each assessment activity, write down **when** that particular assessment takes place. It might be **during** or **after** the course. Also make a note of which of these activities is counted towards the learner's final results or grades.

Formative assessment

What is formative assessment?

Formative assessment is the assessment that takes place during a course or programme of study, as an integral part of the learning process, and as such it is down to the teacher or trainer to design and implement it. It is often informal: that is to say, it is carried out by teachers and trainers while teaching and training. It is sometimes defined as assessment *for* learning. It provides feedback to both teacher and learner about how the course is going: how can learning be improved on during the course? Are the learners doing what they need to do? If not, are the teaching and learning strategies chosen by the teacher or trainer in need of modification?

Usually, when people think about assessment, they mean summative assessment: end-of-term exams, final projects and practical demonstrations, or year-end submission of portfolios. We – and our learners – often think about assessment in terms of being marked out or branded by results that stick with us after our course or programme has finished. Bad memories of assessment in the past can often act as a barrier to participation. One example is described here by Jenny, a trainee English lecturer:

> Had the second week of the access course last night. Quite a good-sized group – fourteen – and all mature learners. I remember talking to my manager last week, and she was convinced that they would be an easy group to take because they all wanted to come back to college, but that didn't last long!
>
> Two of them kept asking about the assignments for the course and it was really disruptive – I was trying to get them to do group exercises based on the chapter they'd read, but it kept coming back to the assignment. In the end I had to spend over half an hour telling them about why I wanted them to do it and how it would work. But David and Pat kept asking about whether it counted and if it didn't, then why should they bother?

The assignment that Jenny has drawn up for her access learners has clearly caused some consternation. So let's have a look at it and see what the issues are:

> **Jenny's assignment:**
> Group: Access to Higher Education – English
>
> This assignment is due in week eight of this term. It will be returned with feedback by week ten. Please make sure that you have read the first five chapters of the set text before starting the assignment.
>
> For this assignment you are asked to answer the following questions:
>
> 1. How does the author illustrate Billy's relationships with his school and his teachers? Choose two incidents to write about.
>
> 2. What do you think Billy's own attitude to school and education is? What do you think are the things that have influenced him in this regard?
>
> Each answer should be no longer than 250 words.

Jenny has set deadlines for submission and feedback, she has set word limits and she has asked specific questions about the book. The question is: why have two of her learners reacted against being asked to do this so strongly? As you can imagine, there are several answers to this question. It may be that both David and Pat are nervous about completing some written work. If this access course is the first formal programme of study that they have undertaken for some time, then we can understand and sympathise with their position – adult learners sometimes find it difficult to get back to completing written work after a period of time away from education. But the real reason may be hinted at in the comments that Jenny noted in her learning journal: if the assignment 'doesn't count', then why bother?

The purposes of formative assessment

The answer may lie in David and Pat's preconceptions as to the purpose of assessment. Unless the assignment is going to go towards their final mark, why should they need to do it? Perhaps they do not see it as relevant, or as a good use of time?

Jenny thought of this, and decided to spend some time in her lesson explaining what she was trying to do:

> I told the group about why I wanted them to do the exercise. It was partly to help them, but partly to help me as well! That made them laugh and relax a little. I explained to the group that by getting them all to do a short piece of writing, it helped me work out how they were doing so far, and whether or not I was getting all the ideas over to them. I also told them that by being asked specific questions, it was good practice for them because it made them start to think about how they needed to analyse the book and not just describe it. Making them do some writing was actually a learning activity, because they would be thinking about the book and using it more actively to find answers to the questions. I told them that I hoped it would help keep them interested as well!
>
> All this took nearly half an hour! Looking back, I'm amazed it took so long. But some of the group wanted to speak and, best of all, David and Pat saw what I was getting at and agreed that it was a good idea!

Jenny has made some excellent points here. She has highlighted the value of the assignment as a learning activity, and as a chance for her learners to show her what they can and cannot do so far. This helps Jenny to plan her future lessons, especially if, after reading the assignments, she sees that there are some issues or ideas that quite a few of the group have not got to grips with. Moreover, by spending time explaining all this to the group, Jenny is involving her learners, helping them to understand why assessment such as this is so important, and how she, as the teacher, will use it. By talking to her group openly about the process, Jenny is breaking down a barrier between the learners and the course. Rather than assessment simply being something that is done to the learner, who becomes a passive recipient of the assessment process, it becomes something in which the learner actively participates and this is encouraging and motivating.

THEORY FOCUS THEORY FOCUS **THEORY** FOCUS THEORY FOCUS **THEORY** FOCUS

Malcolm Knowles and Carl Rogers place a high value on concepts such as 'self-direction', 'self-actualisation' or 'self-evaluation' in learning. These two authors originally focused on adult learning, although defining how old a learner needs to be to be classed as 'an adult' is never straightforward. Many similar ideas have found their way into the post-compulsory education and training sector as a whole, where 'learner-centred learning' is a commonplace expression. We read that learners need to be encouraged to 'take ownership' of their learning, to be 'autonomous' and to 'engage in the learning process'. These strategies are assumed to increase motivation and therefore help increase retention and achievement rates, although this is an area of debate. Irrespective of how accurately we can evaluate the effectiveness of such an approach, however, it has clearly been beneficial to Jenny in re-engaging two learners who were potentially becoming detached from the programme of study.

Jenny's assignment is an example of formative assessment – assessment that is primarily designed as part of the learning process. Assessment can be for learning and can help learning – it is not just about the end-of-term test.

CLOSE FOCUS **CLOSE** FOCUS **CLOSE** FOCUS **CLOSE** FOCUS **CLOSE** FOCUS

Are there any other ways in which Jenny can use the information and feedback that she gathers from the assignment?

We have already looked at initial and diagnostic assessment, and we considered the fact that no system is perfect. Diagnostic assessment tools do not always spot every particular difficulty or barrier that a learner may be facing. Jenny's assignment may be useful in helping her diagnose any particular difficulties that her learners may be experiencing. This may mean referral to a specialist for advice, or it may simply mean that Jenny needs to redesign some of her lessons, activities or resources. Either way, her assignment can be a useful tool for diagnosing problems that have not surfaced before.

To sum up, there are several potential uses of formative assessment that are worth noting:

- **to facilitate learning;**
- **to see whether learning has taken place;**
- **to provide feedback to teachers and trainers on how learners are progressing, clarifying for the teacher or trainer what can be done to improve, extend or enhance learning;**
- **to provide feedback to learners concerning their own progress, clarifying for the learner what he or she needs to do to improve, extend or enhance learning;**
- **to diagnose learners' needs or barriers to learning and help inform any necessary changes to the course or programme of study.**

The application of formative assessment

In Chapter 5, we will be looking at assessment methods in general. Here we will look more closely at methods of formative assessment. Jenny's task is a perfectly good way of going about things, but it is by no means the only way. Let's turn to the learning journal kept by Michael, a lecturer in the engineering department of an FE college. He teaches a range of learner groups: adult learners in the evening, a 14-16 group on Wednesday afternoons, and 16-19 groups for the rest of the time. In this extract, he is writing about a group of learners on an entry-level programme covering a range of basic workshop techniques. Here, the group is beginning work on a particular unit of the course: folding and working with sheet metal.

Hard work today, but rewarding. The learners are all working at such different speeds, it gets really hard to keep up with them. Five of them are all about where I thought they'd be by this stage of term, but the other four are totally different. Two are really good – they know their way round the tools and the workshop, they work well and they've really made good progress with the practical activities. The other two are at the other end of the scale – much slower and still needing more contact time from me. We were in the workshop for two hours this afternoon, and even with time for a break in the middle, I was exhausted – constantly on the go, looking at what they were doing, answering and asking questions and dealing with problems. I had to find extra tasks for the quick ones, but all the others got to where I wanted them to be by the end, although the two slower ones took a lot of effort. It was worth it though: by the end of the day, I had a good idea of how they were all getting on, and knowing about the different speeds at which they are working has helped me plan out the next three sessions in more detail.

Jenny's formative assessment technique is formal, for the following reasons:

- **It was strategically timed as part of her scheme of work.**
- **Formal written feedback was planned, to be delivered two weeks after submission.**
- **A structured, valid activity was set for the learners.**

Michael's formative assessment technique, on the other hand, could be described as informal.

- **It was taking place during the workshop session in an *ad hoc* manner.**
- **Michael's assessment methods (question and answer, observation) were flexible and constantly changing according to the needs of the learner, rather than being fixed in structure.**

At the same time, however, Michael does have a formal task to look after as well: the 'practical activities'. But because he does not describe them in detail in his journal, we do not know what they are for – are these practicals formative or summative assessments? And what difference does this make?

Jenny, similarly, may be using informal formative assessment strategies with her group. When she asks her group questions about what they have read since the previous week, or when she divides them into buzz groups to discuss key topics or ideas, she will be constantly observing and listening to them. The answers they give, the questions they ask, even their body language – all these can help Jenny assess her learners' progress.

CLOSE FOCUS **CLOSE** FOCUS **CLOSE** FOCUS **CLOSE** FOCUS **CLOSE** FOCUS

Consider Jenny's and Michael's learning journal extracts once more. What do their different methods of formative assessment have in common? Do the formative assessments that you use share these characteristics?

One of the most important things that they have in common is that they are both examples of assessment for learning. Both Jenny's formal written assignment and Michael's observations are helping the learning process, by providing encouragement and feedback, and giving learners and teachers opportunities to evaluate how things are going.

The place of formative assessment in the learning cycle

There are many different learning cycles, although David Kolb's *Experiential Learning Cycle* is one of the best-known:

According to this model, formative assessment can be seen as an example of **concrete experience**, just like any other strategy or experience that you may plan and design for your learners. The process of feedback and evaluation can be seen as **observation and reflection** and **forming abstract concepts** – the learner will have to consider the feedback that he or she receives and with the help of the teacher or trainer, decide what to do next. That final stage is one of **testing in new situations**, where the learner tries out what he or she has learned.

Self-assessment and peer-assessment

Kolb's cycle may not be perfect (Peter Jarvis, for example, has argued that Kolb's model is too simplistic), but it does introduce us to our final key issue relating to formative assessment. In the learning cycle, reflection is seen as a key component – just as it is a key component in many teacher-training programmes. If we, as teachers and trainers, are to use Kolb's model (or similar) when analysing our own practice, then we should be encouraging reflective practice amongst our learners as well. In her learning journal, Jenny's account of explaining how the formative assessment process would work can be seen as the first stage in this process: she encouraged her learners to think about why they were completing the assignment, and how they – and she – would be able to evaluate and act upon the results. This evaluation will be communicated through feedback, both written and oral (feedback is dealt with in more detail in Chapter 6). As well as completing their assessment, Jenny wanted her learners to think about both the process and the results of that assessment. This can be seen as a form of self-assessment, where each learner is encouraged to cast a critical eye over their own work. This could take place both before and after the submission of a piece of formal assessed work.

In this piece of reflective writing, Nicky, a workplace assessor, is describing a one-to-one tutorial session. The learner is studying for an NVQ level 2 in Childcare, and has submitted a portfolio-based assignment.

Before I began giving my feedback, I asked Susan how she thought that she had done with her portfolio. I gave her a couple of minutes to think, and then used a few questions as prompts. To begin, I kept things quite general, and asked her about her spelling and grammar and the presentation of the file. This was important because several pieces of work that she had handed in before were poorly presented and full of mistakes, and we had highlighted literacy skills on her action plan. Susan was a little unsure how to begin, I think (and this was the first time that I had asked questions such as this, to be fair) but after a few moments she told me about how she had taken more care and time over her writing than before, although she did find it difficult and was a little discouraged. I thought that she had worked to make real improvements this time, and I told her so, although her literacy skills are a concern, and I may need to get some help about this.

We then spoke about the actual units in question, and I asked Susan about all the different competencies and if she thought that she had achieved them. Susan was a little guarded at first, but soon opened up. I started by getting her to talk about those parts of the assignment that she had enjoyed completing, before asking her about the parts that she found difficult. This was a real eye-opener. The part of the course that dealt with child abuse had proved to be really difficult for her because she found it upsetting. This does happen from time-to-time, and those lessons are always the ones that I have to plan very carefully. But because she had found it upsetting, Susan had really skimped over the assessment and now that she thought about it, she wasn't sure if she had done enough. And she was right – the rest of the file was fine!

Nicky's careful use of questioning techniques has helped Susan to self-assess her portfolio. If she can develop this ability and self-assess all the time – and not just when prompted by her tutor – then Susan will have developed a very useful skill. Refer back to Chapter 2 for more detailed notes on self-assessment.

Another technique that some practitioners use is peer-assessment. This is a form of assessment where members of a peer group (a group of learners in the same class or workshop setting, all attending the same course) assess each other. After all, if learners can learn from teachers and trainers, books and websites, videos and field-trips, they can learn from each other's experiences and knowledge as well. Various strategies for peer-assessment are looked at in Chapter 5. Here are two:

- **Encourage group-based activities within classes. This could lead to a presentation, or a poster display. Each group's display or presentation could be assessed by the other groups using a feedback form that the class as a whole has designed. Asking the class to design the feedback form will help them consider what skills, competences and abilities are important for the course as a whole.**
- **Write up a series of mock-answers to assignments that are similar to those carried out by your learners. Ask the learners to mark them – either individually or in small groups – and then explain to the rest of the class why they marked them the way they did.**

Some learners can be resistant to activities such as peer-assessment and self-assessment, arguing that it is the tutor's job to carry out the assessment. It is understandable that these learners would question the value or reliability of being assessed by their peers. On the other hand, peer assessment and self-assessment are valuable not only because they help learners understand how the assessment process actually works, but also because they prepare learners for real-life situations (in the workplace, for example) where they will not have a teacher or trainer telling them if they have carried out an action correctly.

THEORY FOCUS **THEORY** FOCUS **THEORY** FOCUS **THEORY** FOCUS **THEORY** FOCUS

Kathryn Ecclestone has argued persuasively that formative assessment is often equated with continuous assessment whereas, in fact, they are quite different. Formative assessment is a learning process. Continuous assessment is the systematic accumulation of small summative assessments that may or may not be linked together to form a larger submission, but which all go towards assessing the learning that has taken place at the end of the programme of study.

Summative assessment

What is summative assessment?

Formative assessment is assessment *for* learning, and summative assessment is assessment *of* learning. Teachers and trainers use summative assessment to discover what a learner has achieved during the programme of study. Summative assessment is normally carried out at or towards the end of a course. It is always a formal process, and it is used to see if learners have acquired the skills, knowledge, behaviour or understanding that the course set out to provide them with. It gives an overall picture of performance.

Sometimes, teachers and trainers have to design and mark the work, and we are responsible for making sure that the assessment activities we design are compatible with the curriculum documents we receive from the awarding body, and for making sure that we mark the work according to the criteria that the awarding body gives us. On other occasions, the awarding body (such as City and Guilds, or OCR) dictate how the summative assessment is to be carried out. On these occasions, our responsibility is to implement these assessments correctly, in accordance with procedure.

Each of these situations poses its own problems, irrespective of whether we are new or experienced teachers and trainers. The curriculum can change from one year to the next due to a range of external influences. Changes to aims and outcomes, for example because of the inclusion of a new topic, will necessitate changes to assessment. Very often, as teachers and trainers, we may find ourselves having to get to grips with a whole new assessment regime in a short period of time, or having to design new assessment activities at the start of a new academic year. Or we may find ourselves questioning whether a learner has done enough to pass an assignment when another colleague has decided that the candidate should fail. We shall consider these problems in detail in Chapter 8.

Summative assessment invariably leads to the award of qualifications: grades, diplomas and certificates. There is a bewildering number of qualifications available within the Lifelong Learning sector, and our learners are seeking to obtain them for a number of reasons. For some, a qualification will lead to new employment or changes to existing employment. Others may need a qualification in order to progress to a higher level of educational provision. Yet it is not just learners and tutors who are concerned with the results of summative assessment: employers, award bodies and funding agencies all have an interest in them. Employers rely on qualifications and records of achievement to ascertain the skills and abilities of their new employees. Awarding bodies need to make sure that their qualifications and assessments are being uniformly carried out across the country. And funding agencies (such as the Learning and Skills Councils) want to know that they are receiving value for money.

Qualifications are undeniably important: they act as a form of currency in the employment market, and are used by a variety of bodies (employers and educational/training institutions) to predict the future performance or capacity of the learner.

We can sum up the uses of summative assessment as follows:

- **to record achievement, through the award of certificates and diplomas;**
- **to anticipate future achievement;**
- **to allow learners to progress to higher study (admissions tutors at colleges and universities may use prior qualifications to help learners choose their next course, or perhaps a learner has to pass a particular course before he or she can move to the next level);**
- **to allow learners to enter or progress within the workplace (successful completion of a work-based learning programme could lead to promotion and employers use qualifications as a basis for selection).**

The construction of summative assessment

A range of methods for summative assessment will be explored in Chapter 5. It is worth noting here that the summative assessment for a programme of study or qualification scheme very often consists of a variety of assessment methods. In Chapter 2, we looked at preferred learning styles. When considering assessment, it is worth remembering that learners will respond differently to the assessments that they are asked to complete. Variety of method can help make summative assessment more accessible for the largest possible number of learners. It can also make assessment more **valid** and **reliable**, as we shall see in Chapter 4.

Boundaries between formative and summative assessment

Here is another extract from Jenny's learning journal, from towards the end of the academic year. It raises some potentially tricky issues.

> The examination timetable came out last week, and I gave copies out to the group last night – some of them are getting a little nervous now! I had guessed when the exam would be, based on what happened last year, so I've had lots of time to prepare them for it. I was hoping that all the nerves and jitters would be out of the way now and so I was a little upset that three of them in particular were panicky. I was upset for them – I'm always nervous before exams, and I remember what I was like before my driving test! But if I'm honest, I was also a little disappointed in myself. I worked really hard to prepare all the assignments that we've done last term and this, and I really thought that they'd all got the hang of it. We've done loads of practice papers and all their assignments have been based on old end-of-year papers. I think I must have misread the signals. Perhaps I thought that they were more confident than they really are?

Just as the distinction between formative assessment and continuous assessment is sometimes not clear, so the distinction between formative assessment and summative assessment needs to be carefully maintained. If summative assessment is carried out through collecting smaller pieces of coursework, or through the gradual completion of units which are built up within a portfolio of evidence, surely it follows that this continuous summative assessment can simultaneously act as formative assessment? Learners can receive developmental feedback on each assignment or element before proceeding to the next one, and tutors will be able to benefit from being able to track the learner's progress during the programme, rather than simply waiting until the very end to see how much learning has taken place. As teachers and trainers, we are more than happy to encourage our learners to submit 'draft assignments' or 'fair copies' to be checked through prior to formal submission. But is this automatically beneficial both for our learners or our own teaching?

RESEARCH FOCUS RESEARCH FOCUS RESEARCH FOCUS RESEARCH FOCUS RESEARCH FOCUS

In a research article titled *Summative assessment: the missing link for formative assessment*, Maddalena Taras (2009) puts forward a theoretically informed critique of much previously published work regarding formative assessment, summative assessment and the links between these. Her argument rests on two main platforms. Firstly, she highlights what can be seen as two distinct definitions of formative assessment. One of these relates to teachers' classroom methods, and defines formative assessment as all of those things that teachers do to promote and give feedback on learning. The second definition relates to learners' work, and the use of feedback to identify the gap between a learner's current performance, and the performance that is desired or required. This latter definition, Taras argues, is more akin to summative rather than formative assessment. As such, there is a conceptual confusion over the two terms. Indeed, this confusion can be added to when considering real-world examples of assessment. Many assessment tasks are, arguably, both formative (that is to say, they can be seen as activities planned or enabled by teachers in order to encourage learning) and summative (providing a snapshot of the learner's current competence or knowledge) *at the same time*.

In the previous extract from her learning journal, Jenny described a slightly different issue. Her formative assessments have all been based around past examination papers. Her reasons for doing so are perfectly sound: as well as using the assignments to get to know how her learners are doing, and how well they are learning, the learners can practise the kind of questions that they will receive in their end-of-year examination. This is clearly a sensible strategy. Advice on how to approach testing is always welcome, but looking at a past paper is even more effective in helping us plan for an exam: we can see exactly how the paper looks, how it is constructed and whether there are any specific instructions that the candidates need to follow. The dilemma for Jenny is one of balance. Setting past papers may be good examination practice, but is it necessarily the best strategy to encourage assessment *for* learning?

REFLECTIVE TASK

Think back to your experiences as a learner rather than a teacher or trainer. This could include current or recent experiences on LLUK-accredited teacher-training programmes. To what extent have you experienced assessment **for** learning as opposed to assessment **of** learning? Is it possible for the same task or assignment to have both formative and summative characteristics?

In practice, of course, we can see how the same piece of work can be used for different purposes. If a candidate hands in a piece of work in draft form, the tutor can treat it as formative assessment, offer developmental feedback and then return it to the learner. As busy tutors with little spare time on our hands to design separate formative assessments and activities, it is tempting to use draft submissions like this. The pitfall is that we simply use such submissions to rehearse for the summative assessment, as Ecclestone points out. The other danger is that we let the summative assessment influence the ways in which we teach or train as a whole.

Teaching towards assessment

Let's return to Jenny's learning journal for the final time.

During the first few weeks of the course, there was a lot of discussion about the end of year exam, both in class and during the coffee break. I'd expected this because they were all adults and some of them hadn't been in education for a long time and lots of them hadn't got any qualifications before – John left school at 15 and that was 20 years ago! There was a lot of 'Will this be in the exam?' and 'Will there be a question on this in the exam?' and 'Will we be assessed on this bit?' and 'Will we have to revise all the set texts or can we miss one out?' Looking back, I think that I spent too much time in class starting a sentence by saying 'When it comes to the exam ...' or 'This bit is important for the exam because ...' I think I'd convinced myself that they would all be fine because we'd spent so much time gearing up to the exam itself.

When I was at college doing my A levels, I remember one of our teachers who told us that we should go 'question spotting'. That was when you went through all the past papers to see which topics always came up in the exam. Then you knew the ones to revise for, and you knew which ones to leave out.

THEORY FOCUS THEORY FOCUS **THEORY** FOCUS THEORY FOCUS **THEORY** FOCUS

'One answer to the question "What passes for pedagogy?" in important parts of post-compulsory education, is assessment. It is widely agreed that assessment influences what is taught and how teaching and learning are 'delivered'. There is also widespread belief among educational researchers and practitioners that assessment can and often does constrain rather than enhance learning outcomes'.

Cullen et al. (2002) page 1

This quote sums up Jenny's dilemmas. On the one hand, quite understandably she wants to make sure that her group is as prepared as they possibly can be for their exam. On the other hand, she is now asking herself whether she has gone too far in this direction at the expense of the rest of the course. Jenny has pushed her delivery of the curriculum so far towards the examination, that other important issues may have been overlooked and other teaching and learning activities and strategies may have been passed over.

Researchers, practitioners and inspectors constantly stress the importance of maintaining a variety of teaching and learning activities. If, as tutors, we restrict our choices of teaching and learning activities to exercises that simply rehearse for summative assessment, then we run the risk of failing our learners during the teaching and learning process as a whole. There are other pitfalls as well: working to the assessment can encourage 'bottom-lining' or 'aiming low', when learners concentrate simply on doing the bare minimum needed in order to guarantee a pass.

Summative assessment constitutes a public recognition of achievement, and it should not be a surprise to us that our learners sometimes focus all their attention on the assessment, rather than the course as a whole. Despite what we may know about our learners' motivation, we should also be unsurprised to learn that many of our learners approach assessment with a certain amount of apprehension. When motivating our learners during the assessment process, feedback is particularly important. This will be discussed in Chapter 6.

PRACTICAL TASK PRACTICAL TASK **PRACTICAL TASK** PRACTICAL TASK **PRACTICAL TASK**

Return to the list of assessments that you wrote at the start of this chapter. As you go through each assessment activity, decide which are formative assessments, which are summative assessments, and which may act as both. Is assessment **for** learning as well as assessment **of** learning present in your chosen course or unit?

A SUMMARY OF **KEY POINTS**
In this chapter, we have looked at the following key themes:

> **formative assessment or assessment *for* learning – what it is and how to use it;**

> **summative assessment or assessment *of* learning – what it is and how to use it;**

> **the distinction between formative assessment and continuous summative assessment;**

> **the impact of assessment on planning and designing for teaching and learning.**

At times there is confusion and disagreement about where the boundaries between formative, continuous and summative assessment exactly lie. There are no straightforward answers. But by being aware of the debate and of the ideas and issues, you will be able to reflect on and analyse your own assessment practice, and this in turn will help you to address your learners' needs to the best of your abilities.

Branching options

Reflection

You probably use formative assessment techniques more often than you think. As you watch your learners, listen to their conversations and peer over their shoulders as they work through their tasks for the day, you are constantly assessing their progress. But what are the benchmarks that you use to assess them in this way? Do you have the curriculum outcomes of your programme of study in the back of your mind, or are you assessing them against more personally-constructed standards that draw on your own vocational or professional expertise?

Analysis

Look at some recent lesson plans where you planned for formative assessment. Are you creating or exploiting situations where assessment for learning can be employed? Asking learners to submit a piece of summative assessment, and then getting them to rework and resubmit the task, is not formative assessment: rather than encouraging learning, such techniques simply reinforce the notion of 'teaching to the test', and reducing all the learners' efforts onto the final assessment, rather than the learning that precedes it.

Research

Suggested follow-up reading appears below, but there are other sources to consider as well. Academic journals can provide up-to-date information and ideas about assessment practice and it is worth looking for articles that deal with specific subject areas or learner age groups.

REFERENCES AND FURTHER READING

Cullen, J, Hadjivassiliou, K, Hamilton, E, Kelleher, J, Sommerlad, E and Stern, E (2002) *Review of Current Pedagogic Research and Practice in the Fields of Post-Compulsory Education and Lifelong Learning.* Tavistock Institute.

Ecclestone, K (2002) *Learning Autonomy in Post-16 Education: the politics and practice of formative assessment.* London: Routledge Falmer.

Ecclestone, K (2003) *Understanding assessment and qualifications in post-compulsory education.* Leicester: NIACE.

Jarvis, P (1995) *Adult and Continuing Education: theory and practice.* Second edition. London: Routledge.

Kolb, D (1984) *Experiential Learning.* Englewood Cliffs, New Jersey: Prentice Hall.

Taras, M (2009) Summative assessment: the missing link for formative assessment. *Journal of Further and Higher Education* 33(1) pp57-69.

4
Validity and reliability

By the end of this chapter you should:

- **know how to design assessment tasks that are comprehensively matched onto the topic or competence that is being assessed;**
- **understand the importance of maintaining consistency when assessing learners;**
- **know what quantity of assessment is needed to ensure a fair result and a guarantee of competence or understanding.**

Professional Standards

This chapter relates to the following Professional Standards.

Professional Values

ES2: Assessing the work of learners in a fair and equitable manner.

Professional Knowledge and Understanding

EK2.2: Concepts of validity, reliability and sufficiency in assessment.

Professional Practice

EP2.2: Apply appropriate assessment methods to produce valid, reliable and sufficient evidence.

Ensuring equal treatment in assessment

Many of us can tell stories, or know someone who can, about a teacher at school who had a bit of a grudge against us. We never got more than 6 out of 10 for our homework and the class favourite always got at least 9 out of 10, almost without trying.

Stories like this still circulate but, in fact, the way in which assessment is carried out and monitored means that as long as tutors do their jobs properly, everyone will be treated in the same way. The way we mark and grade work is monitored (as we shall see in Chapter 8), so there is little room for bias amongst teachers and trainers. The assessment activities themselves are carefully constructed so that all the learners who are on the course are treated the same – there is no unfair advantage, however minor. The needs of the course are also taken into account – assessment methods need to match up to the course in question. There is little point in assessing a hair and beauty course with just a three-hour exam.

Making sure that the actual assessment is the right one for the right job is the focus for this chapter, and there are two key concepts that will help us here: **validity** and **reliability**.

Assessment validity

What is validity?

Validity of assessment actually covers a lot of ground. For example, if you gave your learners a multiple choice test and you asked questions that relied on knowledge that you had not covered during class, the test would not be valid. If you were assessing learners in a workshop, and asked them to perform a mechanical task that was not on the syllabus because they would never be asked to perform it in the workplace, the assessment would be invalid. If a group of learners had progressed into employment based on their assessment results, but were found to lack the necessary workplace skills, despite the evidence of their qualifications, those assessments would lack validity. A valid assessment, in brief, is an assessment that covers the course as a whole, uses appropriate real-life methods, is most suitable to the subject or vocational area and helps predict how the learner will perform in the future.

There are five different aspects of validity of assessment to consider. We shall look at each of these in turn, although it is important to remember that we need all these different strands to be pulled together and that, in practice, there is some overlap between the different strands.

Face validity

To guarantee face validity, we need to make sure that the assessment really does assess what it was intended to assess. Are we assessing the particular skills, competencies or body of knowledge that we set out to assess? Has our chosen assessment method measured the growth in understanding, improvement in motorability or change in attitude for which it was selected in the first place?

Content validity

To guarantee content validity, we need to think about the way in which the assessment covers the content of the unit or programme of study. Let us asume that our course outline (a motor vehicle course or a business studies course) gives us eight different objectives. To ensure content validity, our chosen assessment method would have to cover all of those learning outcomes. Within our course, we may have covered a number of different topics. It may not be practicable to include assessments based on all of those topics in depth, so our concern would be to include an adequate sample from across the course, and not to focus on just a part of it. And of course we should not ask questions about topics that have not been covered by the course.

Construct validity

To guarantee construct validity, we need to think about how our assessment has been constructed. If we were assessing learners on a childcare programme, we would not just give them a written test: we would also observe them in the workplace. If we were giving a test to trainee engineers, we would want to test their mechanical skills, spatial awareness and ability to use tools and machinery: how can we assess trainee engineers without getting them to perform the kinds of tasks that, as qualified engineers, they would have to perform regularly? Construct validity relies on the extent to which the assessment is based on, and is appropriate to, the workplace skill or knowledge that we are trying to assess. This will vary according to the competence or vocational area or subject area knowledge that makes up the course. So, a course that is designed to train learners in a new series of mechanical skills would need to be assessed by a range of practical activities. There may be some paper-based assessment as well (for health and safety, for example), but the only way we can properly assess the mechanical skills of the learners is to watch them perform mechanical tasks, not ask them to write a short essay about them.

Predictive validity

To guarantee predictive validity, we need to think about what the assessment tells us – and anyone else who needs to know – about how our learners will perform in their future workplaces and careers. This is important for future employers who, when deciding to offer someone a job based on their qualifications, will need to be sure that the candidate can actually do what the qualification says they can do. If our learners have received their qualification, we need to know that they will be able to use that knowledge or apply that skill or competence in any subsequent context or setting. This may be in the workplace, in another education or training setting or in a home-life context. Alternately, the results of one assessment may be used to predict the learner's potential to obtain future qualifications or participate successfully in further programmes of study.

Validity through authenticity

Finally, we need to consider the authenticity of our assessment methods. Through the provision of work-based learning opportunities, or changes to the assessment methods used in colleges, we need to design and apply assessments to mirror the real-life application of the knowledge or skill that we are testing. An assessment methodology is authentic if it draws on the everyday practice of the occupational area or activity that the course is about. We shall return to authenticity later.

CLOSE FOCUS **CLOSE** FOCUS **CLOSE** FOCUS **CLOSE** FOCUS **CLOSE** FOCUS

Validity is a far-reaching concept in assessment. Spend a few minutes thinking about two different ways in which you have been or will be assessed during the course of your teacher-training qualification – choose one formative assessment and one summative assessment. Consider the ways in which these two methods are valid, using the five headings above to guide your reflections.

Difficulties in maintaining validity

Having analysed some of your own assessment methods, you will have learned that although validity is not in itself a difficult concept, it is something that needs careful attention to detail: as part of a well-planned assessment process, validity should and will come naturally. This is true irrespective of whether we are discussing formal or informal, formative or summative assessment. But there are several ways in which validity can become compromised.

Validity problems
- Wording the question, explaining the task or defining the activity incorrectly can lead to learners performing activities that do not match the course objectives correctly. We need to define carefully the actions, results, evidence or criteria that we are expecting to be performed or met.
- Setting assessments that miss out one or more of the objectives or content areas of the course. Conversely, it is easy to put together an activity that unintentionally includes something that was not part of the course content.

- **Insufficient resources to facilitate authentic assessment** – this can be difficult to organise and expensive to provide, and could relate to equipment, environment or even people. If equipment is lacking, it is often the teacher or trainer who has to take the initiative in planning an alternative.
- **A lack of consistency between teachers or trainers** – the need to guarantee that two or more different assessors come to the same conclusion is a complex issue and will be discussed in Chapter 8.

PRACTICAL TASK PRACTICAL TASK PRACTICAL TASK PRACTICAL TASK PRACTICAL TASK

Read through the following extracts and note down the issues relating to validity that occur.

John is a lecturer in animal sciences at a large agricultural college. He teaches a range of modules, including one that focuses on exotic animals, and his learners are typically seeking careers in either animal care or veterinary nursing. In this extract from his learning journal, he describes the facilities available to him and his learners:

> We have two groups of learners, and for the exotics course they need to do several different tasks. There's a written paper that covers underpinning knowledge, but it covers Key Skills as well. There's also lots of practical work of course, and this will involve handling the animals. So we have a whole section of the college where the animals are all housed and that way we can assess on site rather than having to find placements or something like that. It is laid out just like a proper wildlife park or sanctuary and we have all the equipment that they'd find when they leave college and go to work.
>
> Last year, though, we didn't have the animals. For some of the course, we had to arrange visits to a nearby wildlife park, and we also managed to borrow some animals. When that happened, all the assessments had to be fitted into one day and I think that some of the learners found that stressful. For the rest of the course, the assessments had to be based on written case studies and simulations. It wasn't too bad, but it didn't really work as well because the animal handling is such a practical thing – you need to test it properly, not in the classroom.

Richard has worked as an engineering lecturer for five years. His first job was at a small college where resources were scant and equipment was difficult to procure. During the last few months, he has moved to a larger college, housed in a new building, where the facilities are much more up-to-date:

> At my last college some of the equipment was really out of date – it bore no resemblance to the sort of machinery that they'll be using when they go onto the workshop floor. That pretty well made my job worthless – what's the point in teaching these learners to use kit that they'll never see when they start work? There were lots of core principles of course, and quite a lot of the equipment that we had was good for most of the jobs that they needed to do, but it needs to be up-to-date not only to meet what the industry needs, but to get the learners motivated as well – they do not want to be using antiques. At the new college, it is fantastic. The workshop has been totally refurbished and there's equipment here that I've never used before, so I've got three training days all booked up to get up to scratch!

Jan is an IT lecturer, and teaches a range of beginners' IT courses to adult learners in a community education setting. Her comments on the facilities available at her place of work are less positive:

The room is okay, I guess, although it can be a little crowded. It is fully internet-enabled, and I have a data projector linked to my PC so that I can demonstrate when talking the group through something new. The problem is the age of the machines – they're too old, and as a result they're too slow. Some of the software is okay, but some of it does need updating. The learners get impatient sometimes waiting for things to happen, and so do I.

You may have drawn out some of the following themes:

- **For John, validity is enhanced by the provision of an authentic, realistic environment where assessment can be carried out in a workplace style setting. The previous year, however, the construct validity of the assessment will have been reduced because of the lack of animals.**
- **For Richard, authenticity was a concern at his previous college. At the new college, there is no such problem. In fact, if Richard is to be able to assess his learners, he has to organise some continuous professional development (CPD) in order to stay up-to-date.**
- **For Jan, validity is reduced because the equipment being used does not reflect the reality of the workplace. This leads to frustration for the learners – distractions such as this could 'put them off' during an assessment. This brings us to our second important theme: if the learners are distracted from their task, then the assessment may not be *reliable*.**

Assessment reliability

What is reliability?

Reliability, in the context of assessment, is all about consistency. Is the assessment consistent? Will it work the same way in any place, at any time? If the same person took the assessment twice, would they get the same result each time? In order to guarantee reliability, we need to think about the assessment from two different viewpoints: the learners' and the markers' (remember that, very often, more than one person will mark a piece of work). We shall think about these two viewpoints in turn, although, of course, there is some overlap between them.

The learners

Let us imagine that we have two groups of learners studying psychology. One group consists of full-time learners aged between 16 and 19 who study during the day. The other group is an adult education group who attend classes in the evening. Both groups take the same examination and receive their results a week later. But would it have made a difference if one group had been given an extra day to prepare? If one of the learners was having an operation at the local hospital (a pretty good excuse for missing the test), would he or she have even more time to revise, or would he or she be given a different question paper? And then, would all the other learners complain if they thought that the late candidate was getting an easier paper compared to the one that they had sat?

In theory, it should not matter when or where the learners sit their test. If the assessment is reliable, then it will be completely consistent across the board: whichever college they attend, whoever the teacher is, whenever they sit the test – none of these things should make a difference if the test is reliable.

The markers

If we stay with our two hypothetical psychology groups for a little longer, we can move on to consider their teachers. Would it be fair if each teacher marked his/her own learners' papers? How would we stop one of them showing favouritism? What if we asked each teacher to mark the test papers from the other? Or what if each teacher marked the work that his/her own learners did, but then had all the marking checked by a second marker, or internal verifier (which is just about the same thing)? How will we make sure that each teacher agrees on what constitutes a pass, a merit or a distinction? How will we make sure that each teacher agrees where the dividing line between pass and fail lies?

In fact, if our assessment is reliable, we will not have to worry about any of these problems. Whoever marks the test, wherever they work, if they are given the same piece of work to mark twice, even if they are given exactly the same answers by another candidate – none of this matters if the assessment is reliable.

A checklist for assessment reliability

If an assessment is truly reliable, we can assume the following:

- **The markers or examiners will agree on the mark or grade to be awarded to a given piece of work.** If the assessment is reliable, the same grade or score will be given every time. How this is done will vary between institutions and awarding bodies. Some awarding bodies ask for a sample of learner work to be second-marked. Other awarding bodies ask for all work to be second-marked. Sometimes, the first marking is done by the class tutor, at other times all the learners' work is marked by someone from outside their college. For many qualifications or awards, learners are referred to by a number, rather than by their name: anonymity is thought to ensure fairness. Results from different institutions are compared at both regional and national level, to ensure a level playing field. Second marking also helps spot – and therefore prevent – errors affecting the result. We shall return to these issues in Chapter 8.
- **There will be consistency between the learners' work and the markers' or examiners' grades.** If your learners are working towards a BTEC award, for example, they will be able to achieve a pass, a merit or a distinction. Different criteria are given for meeting these three grades. If the assessment is reliable, then the quality of the learners' work and the grade that it receives should be consistent. Marking schemes help encourage reliability by providing a template for all markers and assessors to work from. However, this is a far from straightforward process. If two examiners agree on the grade or mark to be awarded to a candidate, this may simply be a reflection of the fact that those two examiners both have similar standards in relation to the assessment – it does not automatically follow that they are both assessing the work against an objective standard. The use of marking schemes and marking criteria, normally supplied by the awarding body, will help prevent this.
- **There will be consistency between learners' grades or marks irrespective of where or when they sat the examination or test.** Where a learner has been studying or whenever they are assessed, the results of that assessment should always be consistent. So, if two work-based learners are being observed at the same time, the assessors will be basing their judgement about the learners' competence on the same criteria. If the two assessors switched places, the result would be the same.
- **The language used during the assessment process is clear, unambiguous and inclusive.** Use of language has to be considered in broad terms. Learners will be exposed to a range of written and spoken instructions or resources at different stages of the assessment process: in the written instructions for the test paper or the portfolio activity and in spoken instructions given by an assessor during a workplace visit. The language used in the context of assessment should be inclusive: that is to say, there should be no gender or cultural bias in the questions or instructions;

the task should be clearly explained and, if written down, should have a high level of readability. Instructions and tasks should be explicit and easy to follow.

- The environment in which the assessment will be carried out will not affect the process. We assess our learners in a wide variety of environments – in colleges, the workplace, work-like environments or placements. There is a great deal of variety between all these different settings. A reliable assessment, therefore, will not be affected by the assessment's setting: there should be nothing in the environment that will help, hinder or distract the learner during the task.
- Learners or candidates will not have been coached. This is a tricky area, and needs careful consideration, as coaching has a variety of meanings. In this context, however, coaching is used to refer to any process by which a learner or group of learners is helped to prepare for an assessment activity in a way that provides them with an unfair advantage. For example, a workplace assessor could ask leading questions that spoon-feed the answers to the learner, or could provide so much detailed feedback that he or she is effectively writing the assignment for the learner (feedback is discussed in Chapter 6).

CLOSE FOCUS **CLOSE** FOCUS **CLOSE** FOCUS **CLOSE** FOCUS **CLOSE** FOCUS

Think back to the two assessment methods within your teacher-training programme on which you reflected earlier (page 39). Consider the ways in which the two methods are reliable, using the six headings to guide your reflections. Make a list of any factors that may affect reliability.

Difficulties in maintaining reliability

Reliability is not an inherently difficult concept, but it does require attention to detail across a range of issues. Reliability can be affected by a variety of factors, and we may not always have direct control over them. Summative assessments, for example, are often prescribed by an awarding body, but we still have to implement, manage and mark them. There are lots of potential problems to consider:

- workshop/classroom/workplace environment – physical conditions, distractions, equipment, facilities;
- structure of assessment activity – clarity of instruction, cultural/gender/ethnic bias;
- consistency in marking/examining/assessing;
- motivation of the learner – if the learner perceives the assessment as relevant, their interest will increase (we shall return to this theme in Chapter 5).

CASE STUDY

Performing arts

This case study presents some of the themes in the last two chapters. As you read through it, make notes of the steps taken by the tutor to ensure the validity and reliability of his assessments, and of any factors which may affect validity and reliability.

Richard is a lecturer in performing arts, specialising in acting. He is teaching a group on a BTEC First Diploma in Performing Arts, and has to design an assessment for Unit B6 – Devising Plays. The outcomes for this unit are:

On completion of this unit a learner should:
1 Be able to explore and develop material for a devised play
2 Be able to use a range of drama forms and techniques

3 Be able to communicate ideas, issues and/or feelings through presentation of devised work

4 Understand the effectiveness of devised work for performance.

Richard has already started to plan the summative assessment for this unit. However, he has also decided to design some formative assessment activities to help the group work towards their final performance piece. There is some guidance on content, but Richard has to work out the detail himself.

For now, he has decided to focus on learning outcome 2 and to plan some formative assessment activities. Here is an excerpt from his learning journal:

First diploma group today. We went through the unit and talked about what they would need to do. I decided to start them off with finding material from which they could devise their performance piece. I decided to run a discussion group but it was really difficult – some of them just kept talking and some sort of shrunk into the background. I think that the size of the group was a problem here – if there were still just 15, I bet it would have been easier. The group has felt very different since the classes were merged. A lot of them seemed to be stuck and couldn't think of anything that they would like to use for their devising. I asked them all to come back to the next session with some material that they could use, but only a few of them managed to organise something. So I took matters into my own hands, and prepared materials for them to work from. I also decided to hold rehearsals, and then I could give feedback on these to help with their preparation for the final performance.

Richard decided to draw up a schedule for the group. Before their final performances, which would make up part of the summative assessment for the module, he created a rehearsal timetable, so that each group would be observed and assessed on two occasions before their final performance. These two observations would constitute the formative assessment for the unit. Each rehearsal would be assessed against the criteria for the unit, and then feedback would be given. Final performances would be recorded on video camera, and then played back as part of the feedback and evaluation process. This will allow Richard to view each performance more than once when assessing, and then the tapes can be passed over to the internal and external verifiers. The learners will have had two dress rehearsals prior to their final performance, by which time they will hopefully be confident and fluent in performance. But Richard is in danger of falling into a trap here. As we have seen in Chapter 3, formative assessment can be a valuable method of developing and encouraging learning, but if he focuses too closely on the summative assessment at the end of the unit, he may miss opportunities to engage and develop his group. Richard, like the rest of us, is under pressure to make sure that all his learners complete the unit – and, indeed, the rest of the programme – successfully. We are often made aware of the financial implications of low achievement. But he may well be tempted to spoon-feed his learners, to guide them through practice exercises and directive feedback towards the summative assessment.

What steps did Richard take to ensure validity and reliability?

- Using the unit criteria to create a marking scheme – this will help Richard to assess his learners fairly, because they will all be working towards the same standard.
- Using video to facilitate evaluation – learners can watch their own and their peers' performances and reflect on their activities. Learning outcome 4 explicitly addresses this process, and so the use

of video helps ensure validity.
- Using feedback to facilitate verification – this will help Richard assess. He can watch a performance for a second time and reflect on his marking. This will also allow an internal and external verifier to view the same learners' performances and any discrepancies between assessment can be discussed.

What factors may affect the validity and reliability of Richard's assessment?

- The size of the group prevents Richard from running an effective discussion session – not all the learners can participate. Discussion groups provide a good opportunity for informal, formative assessment, but in this instance it would not be reliable.
- Richard is in danger of coaching his learners if he gives them feedback that simply tells them what they need to do to pass the unit.

Sufficiency and authenticity

What is sufficiency?

Sufficiency of assessment can mean slightly different things, depending on context. When a teacher/trainer is using portfolio-based assessment, sufficiency refers to the amount of material or evidence required to demonstrate unequivocally that a particular learning outcome or criteria have been met. This may involve using a number of different types of evidence (written statements, witness testimonies, written assignments or video evidence). In a module or programme of study where a range of assessment methods are used (such as in the case study above), sufficiency refers to the amount of assessment that learners have to undergo. Very often, learning outcomes are assessed on more than one occasion, and the same activity can be used to assess more than one outcome. At the same time, sufficiency refers to the number of times, irrespective of methodology, that it is necessary to assess learners in order to ensure that learning has taken place.

The need for sufficiency is supported by the concept that a learner needs to demonstrate a new skill or attitude or apply a new body of knowledge more than once in order for the teacher/trainer (or anyone else, for that matter) to be sure that learning has occurred and that competence, mastery or understanding has been reached or acquired. Other stakeholders in assessment, such as employers, also need to know that a potential employee's qualification was not awarded purely on the basis of the candidate having a good day on the day they took the test but on a consistent performance. Conversely, sufficiency of assessment prevents candidates who have a bad day being unduly penalised. In this sense, therefore, sufficiency relates to **reliability**.

What is authenticity?

Authenticity has two quite distinct meanings in assessment. First, it refers to the actual work that is produced by the learner – is it all their own? Courses that are assessed through closed examinations have little to fear in this regard, but cases of cheating or plagiarism are found in continuous assessments. Perhaps a learner has copied material from the internet, and pretended that it is her/his own work. Or perhaps a learner has fabricated a piece of evidence that he or she has submitted in a portfolio.

The second meaning of authenticity is different. It refers to the need, particularly acute in vocational and technical courses of study, for assessments that reflect the reality of the workplace that the learner is preparing to enter. When designing assessment activities, therefore, we need to consider how the skills or competencies that are being assessed would be recognised in the real world of work. Ensuring authenticity involves two key factors:

- **provision of equipment that meets current industry/trade/vocational practice needs;**
- **access to realistic work environments or environments that are designed to mirror the world of work.**

In this sense, therefore, authenticity relates to **validity**.

Practical steps

Validity and reliability are quite distinct characteristics of assessment, although in practice they are inseparable: we cannot apply one without the other. For all of us, summative assessments are planned and delivered according to criteria laid down by awarding bodies. The methods used will sometimes be directed by the awarding body, and sometimes designed by the teacher or trainer, following the criteria that we have received, as we saw in our case study earlier in the chapter. Formative assessment is very much up to us, but still needs careful planning. When choosing an assessment method (examples of different methods are given in Chapter 5), remember the following:

For validity
- **Choose methods that are authentic and appropriate – a cycle mechanic could be assessed on his/ her competence in repairing bicycles using a written assignment, but practical tests would be more suitable from the point of view of the learner, the course and a future employer.**
- **Choose methods that cover all the intended learning outcomes. It may help to draw up a table that lists all the learning outcomes – skills, knowledge or understanding – and then write how and when they will be assessed next to each one. This checklist could then be used ensuring the valid assessment of each learner.**

For reliability
- **Make sure that your learners know when, where and how they will be assessed.**
- **Make sure that you are sufficiently prepared and knowledgeable to assess fairly – have you spoken to other colleagues about standards? Have you taken part in trial marking sessions to prepare you for the real thing? Have you found out how the learners' work will be internally or externally verified? (This is covered in detail in Chapter 8.)**
- **Have you been given or drawn up a marking scheme? This will help maintain consistency and facilitate the work of the internal verifier/second marker.**

Refer to Chapters 5 and 7 for examples of assessment checklists and marking schemes.

A short note about norm-referencing and criterion-referencing

The way that examinations are marked and graded has changed over time. It used to be common for learners to be assessed and graded against the norms of achievement of other learners. That is to say, the assumption was made that out of any group of learners, there would always be a few who were very able and would always get top marks, a few who were not at all able and would fail, and more people in the middle. This would happen whatever the course, whatever the year. Marks would be allocated on a quota. So, the top 10 per cent of the group might get an 'A' and the 20 per cent who came next would get a 'B' and so on, down to the bottom 10 per cent who might get an 'F'.

This system, which is called **norm-referencing** – makes the assumption that we do not 'get better' at learning as a whole, but that there will always be few high-fliers and low-achievers, and more people who are just average. This was seen as a useful system because it helped maintain consistency year-on-year. It did not matter if the test paper was 'harder' one year, because the same percentage of learners would still get a top grade – whatever their actual marks. In theory, if the paper was really easy one year and everybody got at least 90 questions right out of 120 (or 75 per cent), then 10 per cent of learners would still receive an 'F', even though they got three-quarters of the questions right!

Norm-referencing can help identify the cream of the crop, and so it is useful for selection, but it only works if we assume that there are such things as 'typical' learners or groups of learners, and that there will always be the same number of 'high ability' or 'low ability' learners in a cohort. A more equitable system, and the one that is dominant in teaching and training today, is **criterion-referencing**. Here, the specific criteria for success or achieve-ment are set out in advance, and the learners are assessed on the extent to which they achieve them. If the required level of achievement has been met, then the learner will receive the award or qualification.

Criterion-referencing demands reliability, however: the criteria for success need to be applied across the board so that all learners have an equal opportunity to achieve them. This in turn necessitates the creation of criteria that are easily understood by not only all the teachers and trainers who will assess the work, but the learners as well: they need to know what the standards are. The criteria need to be **transparent**, and so to ensure reliability, the learners will need both unambiguous instructions and clear guidelines about their expected achievement. On BTEC courses, for example, the assessment guidelines will tell learners:

- **what they need to do to achieve a pass;**
- **what they need to do to achieve a merit;**
- **what they need to do to achieve a distinction.**

The criteria give us, as teachers and trainers, guidelines for what we expect a learner who achieves a certain grade to be able to do.

So why has assessment practice moved towards criterion-referencing and away from norm-referencing? There are many reasons for this, some of which are quite complex. In part, it is due to the recognition that learners should be rewarded for the work that they do according to the demands of the course rather than according to how well the other members of their group are doing. Assessing the achievement of learners according to criteria allows the use of APEL (see Chapter 2), which provides new opportunities for learners to participate in education. And a more transparent system of marks and awards increases the accountability of educational institutions. Finally, criteria provide a detailed description of requirements for successful assessment, which in turn can be more easily understood by teachers and trainers.

A SUMMARY OF **KEY POINTS**

In this chapter, we have looked at the following key themes:

> **assessment validity (the various ways in which we need to consider validity, and the reasons why);**

> **assessment reliability (why reliability is so important);**

> **some implications of validity and reliability for assessment practice.**

As teachers and trainers in the Lifelong Learning sector, we will encounter an enormous variety of qualification and assessment schemes. Some of us will have to take on responsibilities for assessment design and implementation, and others will have to interpret activities dictated by awarding bodies. But our roles may change: as we progress through our careers, new responsibilities such as second marking or internal verification may well become part of our practice. As such, it is important for us to have a good understanding of these issues, even if our experience of them is limited. Every time we assess our learners – formative or summative, informal or formal, the assessment has to be both valid and reliable.

Branching options

Reflection

Tutors working within formal curricula have much of the thinking related to validity and reliability done for them, with internal moderation and external validation activities organised on a regular basis. To what extent are you conscious of the processes that support validity and reliability within your curriculum? Part-time tutors, and especially those working in adult education, may be less involved in the process. So how do you ensure reliability and validity? And how might this be different from the professional experience of a full-time tutor?

Analysis

Select one summative assessment task that you have recently worked through, or are currently involved in, with a group of learners. Go through your course handbooks or any other curriculum documents supplied whether by the awarding body or by the organisation delivering the course, and track all the ways in which validity and reliability are monitored.

Research

Key concepts of assessment are commonplace features of teacher training literature within the further education sector. Historically, much 'recreational' adult education has not been formally assessed. Now, with the introduction of RARPA (Recognising and Recording Progress and Achievement), more formalised assessment is becoming the norm. Use the internet to find out more about RARPA, how it works, why and where it has been introduced, and why it has been sometimes controversial.

REFERENCES AND FURTHER READING REFERENCES AND FURTHER READING

Cotton, J (1995) *The Theory of Assessment: an introduction*. London: Kogan Page.

Ecclestone, K (1996) *How To Assess The Vocational Curriculum*. London: Kogan Page.

Rowntree, D (1997) *Assessing Students: how shall we know them?* London: Kogan Page.

5

Assessment methods

By the end of this chapter you should:

- **be able to select and evaluate a range of diverse assessment methods;**
- **know how to reconcile assessment methods with curriculum requirements;**
- **be able to evaluate assessment methods in respect of the individual needs of learners.**

Professional Standards

This chapter relates to the following Professional Standards.

Professional Values

ES1: Designing and using assessment as a tool for learning and progression.

Professional Knowledge and Understanding

EK1.2: Ways to devise, select, use and appraise assessment tools, including, where appropriate, those which exploit new and emerging technologies.

Professional Practice

EP1.2: Devise, select, use and appraise assessment tools including, where appropriate, those which exploit new and emerging technologies.

REFLECTIVE TASK

Before reading on, spend a few minutes thinking about your own experiences of being assessed, in any post-compulsory educational context – perhaps a programme of study undertaken at a college or university, or perhaps technical/vocational qualifications that were assessed in the workplace. You may choose to reflect on a current or recent programme of teacher-education. Make a list of the different ways in which you were assessed, when the assessments took place, and the kinds of knowledge, competences or skills that were being assessed. If you were redesigning the course in question, would you change any of these assessment methods?

Assessment in practice

As teachers and trainers in post-compulsory education, we encounter an array of qualifications, curricula and awarding bodies that can be quite overwhelming. The variety of work that takes place in the Lifelong Learning sector – the different subjects that are studied, the different groups of learners and the different ways in which courses are organised (full-time, part-time, work-based, and so on) – are reflected in the range of assessment techniques in use: observations, examinations, computer-based tasks, practical demonstrations and group presentations, to name only a few. We have to remember to choose assessment methods that provide the best fit with the course or programme of study with which we are involved. Our choice of assessment methods will be influenced by our answers to the following questions.

- **Are we planning formative or summative assessment?**
- **Is the assessment formal or informal?**
- **What do we have to do to ensure that the assessment will be valid and reliable?**
- **What do we have to do to ensure that the assessment will be authentic?**

Our freedom of choice regarding assessment will vary according to context. We often have more freedom of choice over formative assessment (assessment *for* learning) compared to summative assessment (assessment *of* learning), although this will depend on the individual course or programme. Many programmes of study use set assignment methods and all the teacher or trainer has to do is follow given procedures: the handbooks or guidance documents supplied by awarding bodies often provide detailed information about how and when assessment should take place. On other occasions, a programme of study gives us a series of learning objectives or outcomes, and we have to design an assessment to fit. For many adult education tutors, a considerable degree of professional autonomy is allowed, and assessment methods, perhaps even assessment outcomes, may be left entirely at their own discretion. Sometimes, particularly if we have a learner with a specific learning need or disability (Chapter 9), we may need to arrange for an assessment that differs from the method set down by the awarding body. For some programmes of study, it may be possible for a learner to negotiate an assessment method that is different from the 'standard' format. In short, despite the fact that we do not always have control over how we assess our learners, particularly when it comes to summative assessment, we still need to be aware of the range of methods available to us.

Assessment methods

Examinations

Mention of an examination invariably conjures up a mental image of a large hall filled with row after row of desks, with examination candidates furiously writing away for two or three hours. Closed examinations, as they are called, are still very much part of the PCET curriculum, although they are not as widespread as they used to be. Examinations do have their uses: they are very effective at assessing a specific body of knowledge, as well as assessing more generic study skills (organising ideas, constructing an argument or solving a particular problem). And of course it is important to remember that the exact format of the exam can vary – several of the assessment methods that appear below can be found in examination situations as well as in classrooms. For example: an exam paper can consist of essay questions, or short-answer questions, or a mixture of both.

Examinations can be found in a variety of guises. As well as the 'traditional' closed paper (when candidates have a fixed time-limit in which to answer a number of questions based on their recall, memory and understanding), examinations can also be 'open-book' (where candidates can take books or notes into the examination room) or 'open' (where candidates collect a paper and take it away, submitting their answers by the end of an agreed period). These two variations on the traditional examination theme can be effective in combating nerves, often cited as a difficulty for learners during exams, and increases the reliability of the overall assessment. Open or open-book exams are more authentic – in real-life, after all, we often get the opportunity to look an answer up when asked a question. Examinations can also be found in a workshop or workplace context, where candidates have been given a specific period of time to complete a particular task or action.

Examinations are commonly used for summative assessment. They can also be used for formative assessment: a lesson-based examination, for example. Examination practice can be a helpful technique in preparing learners for appropriate summative assessment: as well as helping nervous candidates, 'mock' examinations can also help learners acclimatise to examination conditions and practise appropriate techniques (timing, paying attention to instructions, etc.) that can also increase reliability. However, it is important not to reduce such exercises to 'coaching'.

Essays

Essays are commonly found in those courses or programmes of study in the cognitive domain, for example sociology or English. Essays allow learners to demonstrate their knowledge and understanding of the subject matter, demonstrate a range of transferable study skills, such as academic writing, problem-solving and creative or original thinking. They are used both for formative assessment, during a programme of study, and for summative assessment, during end-of-year examinations.

Setting an essay question might seem to be a relatively straightforward exercise. In fact, essays have their drawbacks. It is difficult to set a title that covers anything more than a fragment of the curriculum content at any one time, so depending on the exact format of the assessment, learners might not be assessed on all of the syllabus. This would affect validity. Giving feedback (covered in detail in Chapter 6) can be time-consuming, and maintaining objectivity when marking can be difficult, which in turn affects reliability. This problem can be overcome through the use of marking schemes: for example, a fixed number of marks may be awarded for each of a number of criteria, such as 'structure', 'use of argument and analysis', 'factual/knowledge content', and 'spelling and grammar'. So if, for example, a learner's essay was well presented and full of detail although lacking in analysis, the marks awarded would still reflect the progress made in those areas. And by constructing a feedback form that also covered these headings, specific guidance could be given about the areas of essay writing that need further development.

Essays can be off-putting: nervous learners who lack self-confidence, or who are returning to formal education after a long gap can find it difficult to get used to essay writing. This will affect reliability. Short-answer questions or learning journals, can be an effective alternative for groups of adult returners.

Short-answer questions

Within subjects that are best suited to written assessment, short-answer questions can solve some of the problems raised by essays. Rather than being faced by a single all-encompassing essay question (where the consequences of misunderstanding a question could be catastrophic), a series of short-answer questions provides a more structured framework for the learner to follow. This can help build learners' confidence in attempting written work and reduce the risk of misunderstanding the task, therefore increasing reliability. Marking is also a little more straightforward. Shorter, specific questions can be marked with the aid of a model answer sheet, and marks or grades can be awarded for each component. Careful question choice can also ensure wide coverage of the syllabus, which further enhances validity.

The real drawback of a short-answer exercise compared to an essay is in the level of analysis and detail: it is much easier to encourage detailed, critical work in a longer essay-style format rather than in a short-answer assessment, which runs the risk of being more trivial by comparison. In this issue, as with so much else, the context of the assessment should be your guide. For learners on a level 2 programme, a short-answer paper may be entirely suitable to the aims and outcomes of the course. For a programme at level 4, the opportunity to write a detailed essay may be preferable.

Multiple-choice questions

One way of solving the curriculum-coverage problem is to set a multiple-choice question-naire. With a questionnaire, it is possible to cover a large body of knowledge or understanding quickly and thoroughly, simply by setting at least one question for each topic covered in the syllabus. The questions can be structured in a number of ways – asking for a true or false answer, or giving four possible answers and asking the candidate to select the correct response. It is easy to pitch questionnaires at different levels simply by making the questions more demanding, and questionnaires are both easy and quick to mark, irrespective of the difficulty of the questions. Multiple-choice questionnaires can be both valid and reliable.

Multiple-choice questionnaires can easily be marked by the learners themselves and so are very valuable for self-assessment and peer-assessment. Peer-marking exercises can stimu-late debate about the assessment activity by itself, for example by exploring how or why a wrong answer was arrived at. This can be done as soon as the assessment has been completed, providing very fast feedback as well as a further opportunity for revision and reinforcement of learning.

The major disadvantage of the multiple-choice questionnaire is the time it takes to prepare – it is all too easy to produce a questionnaire that is trivial and lacks rigour. Constructing the test and checking all the answers is a lengthy process. Of course, the learners will always be able to make a lucky guess at the answers, which will reduce both validity and reliability.

Case studies

Case studies can be used in a number of ways: in examinations or classrooms; as part of a short-answer or multiple-choice assessment, or as part of a written report. Case studies provide learners with an example or series of examples drawn from everyday or workplace practice. A case study can appear in a range of formats: a single piece of writing describing a scenario, a collection of documents relating to a particular aspect of workplace activity, or a video recording of an event or series of events, perhaps supported by printed materials. Learners have to respond to a series of questions about the case study, using the attitudes, knowledge or competencies that they have acquired during the programme of study. For example, a case study for a childcare course may consist of a description of an incident that takes place in a 'typical' relevant setting (such as a small child accidentally hurting them-selves during a play session). Candidates go on to answer a series of questions relating to health and safety, how they would help the child, who would have to be informed of the accident, and so on. Case studies such as this are highly effective in maintaining relevance to the occupational area under discussion, and as such are highly authentic forms of assess-ment, which in turn ensures validity.

The marking of such case studies will depend on how the questions are constructed: questions that require essay-style answers will provide the learners with more opportunities to demonstrate deep levels of knowledge and understanding, but may be difficult to mark compared to short-answer questions where model answers can be supplied.

Written reports
Common subjects for written reports include work placements, field trips and practical activities. When accompanying practical or hands-on activities, written reports provide an opportunity for learners to demonstrate relevant underpinning knowledge and to reflect on the activities that they have carried out. This reflection is an aid to self-assessment (or, in the language of Key Skills, improving own learning and performance). A report could be a single piece of writing, or a series of statements broken down through the use of sub-headings or open-ended questions, drawn from the course syllabus. For example, a learner on a health-care course might be asked to write a report about their time in the workplace, based on a number of sub-headings such as 'administrative duties', 'health and safety issues' and so on. A structure like this would give the learner the opportunity to link their experiences in the workplace to the course content and would help enhance the validity of the report.

Learning journals
Reflective practice is a commonly found component of teacher-education programmes within the PCET sector. Learning journals (or diaries or logs) are a common format for such reflection, and are often present in subject areas such as healthcare or counselling where changes in attitude (the affective domain) as well as knowledge or competence are important. They are valuable as a form of self-assessment, but maintaining validity and reliability can be difficult. They can also be effective in encouraging learners who have been away from formal education for a long time to begin writing.

If a learning journal is highly structured, based on questions and sub-headings, relevance to the learning outcomes of the course can be maintained. If the journal is unstructured and written in a 'free-form' style, maintaining relevance can be more difficult. Journals can also be difficult to mark, especially if unstructured, and time-consuming to write.

Projects
Projects work well for individuals and groups. A small-scale research project based around a specific topic, issue or question drawn from the syllabus can be particularly effective. It is often possible to allow learners to choose or negotiate a topic for research, something that can increase motivation and interest. Learners then carry out independent research and present their findings through a presentation to the rest of the group, through creating a poster or writing a report. Projects encourage independent self-directed study, peer-colla-boration, peer learning and creativity and are adaptable to all academic, technical and vocational programmes of study.

However, projects are deceptively time-consuming for the teacher or trainer to prepare and structure. Instructions must be explicit and unambiguous; time-limits need to be realistic; resources may need to be examined in advance; access to research materials in print or on-line may need to be evaluated before the project begins and ways of assessing progress during the project itself need to be considered. It is important that learners do not start to think that a project is a way of getting them to do all the work while the teacher or trainer takes it easy. Explain to the group how and why they should do the project so that the value of the activity can be made explicit, and explain the teacher's role in observing progress, offering support and feedback during the research stage as well as at the final report stage.

Presentations

Asking learners to prepare and give presentations can be a valuable way of assessing a range of abilities and competences. As well as the assessment of the actual subject matter (the 'content' of the presentation), the teacher or trainer can also assess a number of generic or transferable Key Skills, such as communication, or use of IT. The teacher or trainer will need to draw up a marking scheme for presentations based on criteria similar to those used for an essay. Assuming that care is taken over the setting of the questions and their marking, reliability and validity should be high. Presentations are also a good opportunity for self-assessment and peer-assessment. However, care must be taken with peer-assessment. It is too easy to lapse into a cycle of bland and worthless feedback because learners are afraid of giving offence. In order for peer feedback to be constructive, the creation of a feedback checklist is recommended (see Chapter 6).

Nerves are often a factor in presentations. Any kind of public speaking can be a nerve-wracking experience, and nerves can affect the reliability of the assessment. Practice and a supportive peer group will help.

Interviews, orals and verbal assessments

As teachers and trainers, we often assess the knowledge and understanding of our learners simply by talking to them. Otherwise, we can assess their progress during a case study exercise, practical task, or project-based exercise by listening both to their conversations and to the questions they ask the tutor and each other. Assessment based on talking to and listening to learners can be formal or informal. If it is formal – an interview, for example – reliability and validity can be ensured through careful planning. The use of a standard list of questions or interview pro-forma can ensure consistency between interviews and broad curriculum coverage, and the recording of the interview (on audiotape or videotape) will allow a second opinion to be given.

Observations

Talking and watching our learners at work are underestimated forms of assessment. In fact, formal observations are widely used within the Lifelong Learning sector. Observations in the workplace, workshop or other authentic setting are commonly found in a wide range of curriculum areas. Like many other assessment methods, the use of an observation pro-forma listing specific criteria or competences (for example, 'communication skills', 'problem-solving', 'use of tools or machinery') can ensure validity. Reliability is a little trickier, and before carrying out an observation, a teacher or trainer may well have to take part in appropriate professional training. Here again, internal and external verification can help maintain consistency and enhance reliability.

Observations have value beyond such formal contexts, however. Careful attention to learners' behaviour, manners, body language or actions can be as fruitful a form of informal formative assessment as an impromptu question-and-answer session.

Practical tasks, simulations and work-based activities

Realistic, authentic practical tasks need to be arranged within programmes of study where the aims and outcomes of the programme are predominantly concerned with the practical application of skills, knowledge or understanding.

Practical tasks and activities can find their way into many subject areas: technical, art- or craft-based programmes, and science and technology programmes are the more obvious but it is worth remembering that practical tasks can be usefully employed within other curriculum areas as well. Such activities as putting together poster displays, creating hand-outs or other resources, making videotape or audiotape recordings, organising and participating in artistic ventures like theatre performances can all be engaging, authentic and relevant both to the curriculum and to the learners.

Portfolio-based assessment

At its simplest, a portfolio is a collection of documents, materials or other work produced by an individual learner during her/his time spent studying any programme or course. Because of this, a portfolio will mean slightly different things to different people, depending on the course. For an art and design course, a portfolio could include technical drawings, sketches, notes made while researching particular artists or artistic techniques or photographs. For a competence-based course or qualification, a portfolio would include all the evidence that the learner has collected to demonstrate that a particular competence has been learned or acquired, including reports from workplace observations, notes from interviews, witness testimonies, documents or other artefacts generated in and/or for the workplace by the learner.

The creation of the portfolio is very much the responsibility of the learner, invaluable for generating interest, enthusiasm and ownership. A portfolio will also encourage self-assessment and reflection: by analysing and reviewing the material, the learner can revisit their experiences. Assuming that the different components of a portfolio are carefully linked to specific objectives or outcomes, assessment validity is high. For work-based qualifications, portfolio material is often drawn directly from, or modelled on, workplace practice, ensuring authenticity. And portfolios are second-marked to ensure reliability. Portfolio compilation and assessment can be time-consuming and bureaucratic, however: for some qualifications, the sheer volume of evidence required and the time taken to arrange it physically in a file can be off-putting. There is also a danger that the search for sufficient evidence can lead to a rather mechanistic approach to portfolio building where the physical collection of evidence takes precedence over reflection.

> **PRACTICAL TASK** PRACTICAL TASK **PRACTICAL TASK** PRACTICAL TASK **PRACTICAL TASK**
>
> Read through the following extracts from learning journals, and make notes about the assessment methods and activities described.

John is a lecturer in engineering, teaching on a range of City and Guilds programmes.

For the sheet metal fabrication unit, I decided to design my own activity. The course documents listed the specific actions that the learners would have to be able to carry out, the tools and equipment that they would have to use, and so on. Rather than just making some test pieces, I decided to get the learners to make a rack for holding either CDs or DVDs, and they could choose which they wanted to do. I just had to make sure that I designed the activity to match up to all the outcomes. I produced a handout with the template for the two racks on it, and copied it to a transparency as well so that I could use the OHP when explaining what I wanted them to do. It took a little longer than I thought it would (one extra week) but that wasn't too much of a problem. And it was easy to borrow a digital camera so that we could photograph them all and include the photos in the learners' portfolios.

Lynne is a tutor specialising in adult literacy. Here, she is describing an assessment activity from a literacy session for learners on a stonemasonry course who were also working towards a literacy qualification.

> At the start of the course, things didn't go too well. I spoke to the group and they said that they didn't really see the point of a lot of the work that I was asking them to do – it just wasn't relevant to them. They didn't really want to be doing literacy at all – they were just focused on their masonry course. Previously, I'd got material for the exercises from newspapers, or from textbooks or sometimes the internet. What I started doing was finding material that was relevant to their NVQ award.
>
> For one session, I had planned a class-based comprehension exercise where they would have to read a newspaper or magazine article and write a summary of it. Instead of the current affairs article I had originally planned to use, I found an article about how types of buildings and building materials varied according to which part of the country they were found in, and how the availability of local stone would influence building techniques. This turned into a really enjoyable session: many of the group had worked in different parts of the country, and several of the issues raised in the article were similar to their own experiences.

Nigel is a tutor in sports science, and also teaches on a pre-entry to uniformed services programme. Here, he describes an assessed session in the sports hall.

> The examining body sets down all the criteria for physical activities: I don't need to set the assessments at all for this. It provides detailed instructions on how to run the exercises, and the assessment itself is all on audiotape. My role is to explain to the group how the assessment will work, what they need to do and when according to the instructions on the tape, and complete a checklist for each candidate. The checklist comes from the awarding body too. It just lists all the different competences – the physical exercises and tasks – and all I have to do is put a tick if the competence has been achieved, and a cross if it hasn't. Then I collect the checklists, make sure that they are all numbered, and send them off for marking.

Alison teaches computer classes for beginners at her local library. These classes are run on an open learning basis: learners are free to arrange their own times to attend in the ICT workshop, and Alison's role is to set up activities, prepare resources and deal with problems on a one-to-one basis. Here, she describes a number of assessment methods used in her sessions.

> Obviously the assessments are all computer based, but there are some differences. For some modules, I am given four different assignments, and the learner just chooses a number from one to four – they don't know exactly what the assignment will be, but it will always cover the important components of the module – certain functions of a database or a spreadsheet, for example. Increasingly, the learners have to complete assignments online as well. The assignment is set, completed and marked over the internet. The learners are even responsible for logging in to the assignment themselves – I don't mark them or give feedback at all. I thought that this was fantastic at first, and I do still like the fact that I save so much time. But I miss being able to see how they've done and how much they've learned – just getting a 'pass' or 'fail' doesn't tell me as much.

Activity feedback

John realised that simply asking his learners to fold and press some offcuts of metal, whilst meeting the outcomes of the unit, would not be interesting or inspiring. By finding an alternative activity – making a CD or DVD rack – John has kept to the outcomes, ensuring validity, but has also designed a task that will engage the learners, enhancing reliability. He produced a handout and a transparency for the overhead projector to help explain the activity clearly. This is also good practice. Ensuring reliability also requires the learners to understand exactly what is required of them, and by using handouts and an OHP, John has met quite different learning styles – some learners work best with a handout to follow, and others prefer to be talked through an on-screen display. Obviously, a CD rack cannot fit into a portfolio of evidence, but a photograph can. John has displayed initiative and creativity in planning for photographs to be taken.

Lynne has been similarly creative: for her literacy group, the issue of relevance was parti- cularly acute. By redesigning her activity around materials that were directly relevant to her learners' occupational background, she has generated a relevant and authentic task. She also noted that several of the learners made contributions to the session, drawing on their own experiences. This has proved to be an effective exercise in encouraging participation, and the discussion generated provided Lynne with another opportunity for formative assess- ment.

Nigel's example is different again. His is an assessment planned entirely by the awarding body: Nigel's role is to explain the activity to the group, observe their actions and record the results on checklists that are sent back to the awarding body. The question to ask here is: how can we ensure consistency and reliability of assessment? If a different tutor observed the session, would the results be the same? The answer is two-fold. First, the use of a checklist of competences provides Nigel with specific criteria to look for and assess. Second, Nigel will have received training in how to assess through observing, and may also be moderated – that is, observed by a third party while he observes a group of learners. Exercises like this help ensure that different observers are all looking for the same thing.

Alison's learners are asked to complete a variety of assessment exercises – some are assignments in written form, others are completed online. These are both good examples of authentic assessment that is suitable to the curriculum. Alison acknowledges that the internet-based assessments save time, and this is a fair point: designing assignments and giving feedback are time-consuming activities and teachers and trainers have lots to do. But Alison's comments about feeling removed from the assessment process highlights a differ- ent issue, which is the fact that assessment is an integral part of both teaching **and** learning: how our learners perform can be useful to us in evaluating both the assessment and our teaching.

CASE STUDY

Level 1 Certificate and Diploma in Work-based Horse Care

This case study follows Wendy, a tutor in equine studies, as she manages the assessment portfolios of her learners on a level 1 course.

Wendy teaches a range of equine courses at a large rural FE college that offers other courses within the land-based industries curriculum. In common with many of the other courses offered there, the level 1 Certificate and Diploma in Work-based Horse

Care uses portfolio-based assessment. Learners are given a learner guide and logbook at the start of the year and use the templates within them to organise their portfolios through cataloguing the different kinds of evidence that they, with the help of their tutors, have compiled during the course. Examples of appropriate evidence include witness testimonies, documents generated as a result of engaging in authentic working practice, written reports of questioning sessions, statements from employers, and such like. The course documentation tells Wendy – and her learners – which units they need to achieve, depending on the qualification that they wish to work towards. Learners working towards the Certificate need to obtain 28 credits; Diploma learners need 41. Within their portfolios, the learners need to collect different kinds of evidence that shows that they have met the requirements for each unit. The units in turn are linked to national occupational standards (in the same way that CertEd/PGCE/DTLLS assessments are linked to the LLUK standards). National occupational standards are developed by Sector Skills Councils (SSCs): the relevant SSC for this qualification is Lantra – the SSC for Land-based and Environmental Industries.

Unlike the majority of her colleagues at the college who studied for their CertEd/PGCE/ DTLLS on a part-time basis, Wendy did her teacher training on a full-time basis before gaining this, her first post. As such, although she has read much about how portfolio-based assessment works, she has little practical experience. Nor does she hold an A1 Assessor Award (although this is not in fact a problem, as the awarding body does not require tutors to have an A1 qualification). In her continuing professional development (CPD) learning journal, which she is keeping as part of her QTLS professional formation process, she writes about some of the issues that the portfolio process raises:

> It's week six and most of the learners have started to collect quite a lot of evidence, but I'm not sure that they are building their files yet. After my departmental meeting, I spoke to my line manager and she suggested that I book a classroom and get everyone to bring in what they have so far. Then I can sign off some of their units and make a list of who has completed which unit. What I don't know at this stage is how much material they will need to include inside their portfolios. So at the moment the critical issue for me to consider is the validity of each portfolio – and how much evidence will be sufficient to show that a competence has been demonstrated appropriately so that units can be signed off. So I am going to speak to our external verifier in order to get some advice as to how much evidence is required for each unit.

Wendy's approach here is quite common: portfolio building can be a difficult job, and although many of the documents produced by awarding bodies state that learners are intended to 'take ownership' of the assessment and portfolio process (whatever that might mean), the reality is that learners are often confused, rather than helped, by the extensive (or perhaps excessive?) paperwork that they are required to navigate through. Therefore, by holding a portfolio-building workshop, Wendy can talk her learners through the process and explain what they need to do to evidence achievement within each unit. She will also be able to flag up any areas where students are having difficulty in generating authentic evidence, should a simulation be required (which under awarding body regulations is permissible if learners cannot generate evidence to demonstrate competence in any other way).

A SUMMARY OF **KEY POINTS**

In this chapter, we have looked at the following key themes:

> **methods of assessment;**
> **matching methods of assessment to different curriculum areas.**

As teachers and trainers, we will often encounter assessment in a variety of formats that are dictated by awarding or examining bodies. At other times, we have to choose the assessment methods ourselves. Knowing how and when to use a range of assessment methods, irrespective of the freedom of choice that we enjoy, helps us to implement, evaluate and give feedback from assessment. And, perhaps most importantly, we need to know how the assessment works in order to explain it to our learners.

Branching options

Reflection

What methods do use you for formative assessment? Why did you choose them? For many teachers, aspects of our teaching repertoire reflect our own experiences as learners both in terms of strategies that we do use, and strategies that we avoid.

Analysis

The creation of summative assessment tasks is more or less under the control of any individual tutor, depending on a number of factors including the requirements of a curriculum; awarding body regulations; and organisational policies. How much autonomy do you have over summative assessment, and what helps or hinders this freedom of action?

Research

Assessment methodology is a focus for research, located in a range of academic journals such as *Studies in the Education of Adults*, the *Journal of Vocational Education and Training*, and *Assessment and Evaluation in Higher Education*. Many colleges and universities have subscriptions that allow you to browse journals such as these on-line. Do some web-based research, and explore the extent to which your curriculum or sector is represented in current research. If you can, download an article or two and consider how such research can help you make sense of your assessment practice.

REFERENCES AND FURTHER READING

Brown, S, Race, P and Smith, B (1996) *500 Tips on Assessment*. London: Kogan Page.

Gronlund, N E (1991) *How To Construct Achievement Tests* fourth edition. London: Allyn and Bacon.

Habeshaw, S, Gibbs, G and Habeshaw, T (1993) *53 Interesting Ways To Assess Your Students*. Bristol: Technical and Education Services.

Equine National Occupational Standards can be found at:
www.lantra.co.uk/Standards-and-Qualifications/NOS/Equine-NOS.aspx

Curriculum documents relating to the Work-based Horse Care case study can be downloaded from:
www.nptc.org.uk/qualifications/default.asp?area=128

6
Feedback

By the end of this chapter you should:

- be familiar with a range of practical strategies for giving feedback;
- understand key principles of feedback construction;
- understand the role of feedback in the assessment process;
- be aware of the importance of feedback in maintaining learner motivation.

Professional Standards

This chapter relates to the following Professional Standards.

Professional Values

ES4: Using feedback as a tool for learning and progression.

Professional Knowledge and Understanding

EK4.1: The role of feedback and questioning in assessment for learning.

EK4.2: The role of feedback in effective evaluation and improvement of own assessment skills.

Professional Practice

EP4.1: Use assessment information to promote learning through questioning and constructive feedback, and involve learners in feedback activities.

EP4.2: Use feedback to evaluate and improve own skills in assessment.

What is feedback?

Feedback describes the dialogue between the teacher or trainer and the learner and is an integral part of the assessment process.

The tutor's role (in part) is to find out how much the learner has actually learned. What new skills have been acquired? What new knowledge has been mastered? If assessment is the tool that teachers and trainers use to measure learning, then feedback is an associated tool with which we can carry out two important tasks.

1. We can let our learners know how well they have done. This can be an enjoyable experience: it is always pleasant to be able to tell a learner that they have mastered a new skill to the required standard, or demonstrated knowledge and understanding to the required level.
2. Feedback provides us with an opportunity to provide advice, support, ideas or anything else that may be appropriate for learners who have not yet reached the competence that they are working towards, or who have not yet fully understood the body of knowledge that they are studying.

However, just because our learner has already passed the course or been awarded credit, this does not mean that the feedback that he or she receives should be restricted to a bald statement such as 'Well done, you've passed'. By the same token, a learner who has not yet met the required standard deserves more than 'Sorry, you've failed. Try again after you've done more preparation'. Feedback should always be seen as a developmental or formative process, helping the learner to work towards a qualification or award, or helping the learner as they progress to the next stage of their learning career.

Just as assessment can be found in a variety of forms – formative, summative, formal, informal – so feedback can also be found in a wide range of contexts. Formal written submissions are often returned to the learner with written feedback using a form that has been designed by the awarding body. Formative written assessments may be accompanied by feedback that uses an official feedback form, or perhaps a form designed by the tutor. A learner may receive feedback from a workplace observation during a subsequent meeting or tutorial with the teacher or trainer, or in a written report, or both. When doing a small-group learning activity in the classroom, the learners will receive feedback from the tutor as he or she watches, and comments on, their progress. Despite this variety, we can draw out several key themes and issues that should underpin feedback in all its forms.

Why give feedback?

At one level, this is a pretty easy question to answer: we give feedback because learners need to know how well they are doing. If our learners have not met the required standard, they need to know why. If they have met the required standard, they need to know how they did it so that future performance can be ensured. Feedback can help learners repeat their achievements.

When we start to think about learning and assessment a little more deeply, however, more complex issues start to surface. In Chapter 1, we discussed the idea that assessment can be a powerful tool in motivating learners. If feedback is an integral part of assessment, then the role of feedback in motivating our learners should also be considered. Positive feedback can be seen as a reward for learning: confirmation from the tutor that the learner has grasped a new skill or mastered a new body of knowledge.

A checklist for good feedback

This checklist consists of six key principles that relate to feedback in any context – written or oral, vocational or academic. Feedback should be:

1. clear and unambiguous;
2. specific;
3. supportive, formative and developmental;
4. timely;
5. understood;
6. delivered in an appropriate environment.

REFLECTIVE TASK
REFLECTIVE TASK

As you read through the detailed explanation of this checklist, reflect on the issues raised in the light of your own experiences of receiving feedback as a learner. These experiences may be drawn from any prior occupational, vocational or academic qualifications. You may even wish to reflect on your experiences of a current programme of teacher training. How do you think that your current or future practice as a teacher or trainer might be influenced by your experiences as a learner?

1. Feedback should be clear and unambiguous

It is important for the language we use when giving feedback to be clear, concise and easy to follow. It would be pointless to spend time carefully writing assessment guidelines that can be easily understood if we then produce written feedback that leaves our learners unsure about the steps they need to take next. Feedback needs to be straightforward and written in everyday language, and if we do need to use more specialised language (technical terms, for example), we must ensure that the learner understands what the words used mean, and that the learner understands what actions (as appropriate) are needed to develop or improve their performance.

2. Feedback should be specific

Telling a learner that he or she has produced a polished and well-organised portfolio or a well-turned chair leg offers the teacher or trainer a good way to open the feedback dialogue. More specific comments relating to exactly what is so good about the portfolio or the chair leg are more effective in reinforcing existing good progress and achievement. On the other hand, telling the learner that his/her essay is too general and 'fails to answer the question', or that a lighting circuit has been wired up 'incorrectly, so take it apart and do it again' does not provide much help at all. The learner needs to know in what way the essay is too general and exactly what he or she needs to do to answer the question, or exactly where a mistake has been made in wiring up a circuit and which parts of the circuit need to be changed in order to meet the required technical standard.

Good feedback should therefore refer explicitly to the criteria or learning outcomes that are at hand. If the purpose of an essay-based assessment is to fulfil specific criteria, then the feedback should explain the criteria that have been lost sight of, rendering the essay too general and lacking focus. If there is just one technical detail that is preventing a practical assignment from meeting the required standard, then the feedback needs to address that detail. This is not to say that general comments are unwelcome, as they do provide a useful way of starting a discussion with the learner. But general comments need to be followed by more specific and constructive advice.

Very often, an examining body or awarding body will provide a standard feedback form that must be used for a specific course or programme of study and these forms are increasingly divided into sections, each with a sub-heading relating to one of the criteria for the course. These forms make it very easy for tutors to provide specific, focused feedback. On other occasions, it may be necessary to design a feedback form from scratch.

3. Feedback should be supportive, formative and developmental

Good feedback should allow the learner to build on his/her past successes and at the same time move away from errors in understanding or mistakes in technical execution. It is all too easy to reduce feedback to a simple list of the actions necessary to ensure a pass (an 'instrumental' approach to feedback) without properly explaining why these steps are necessary as part of the broader learning experience. Similarly, it is easy to write 'good' in the margin of a written paper (and even easier just to put a tick) with no explanation of what in particular has been done well.

A cursory approach to feedback diminishes its potential to act as a tool for learning. Feedback that accompanies a correct answer, and explains how and why this correct answer has been reached, will reinforce the learning that is associated with the answer. Feedback that accompanies a wrong answer needs to explain how and why the answer is wrong, rather than merely supplying the right answer.

4. Feedback should be timely

For feedback to be effective, it needs to be given as quickly as possible after the assessment activity. The exact timing of feedback will depend on several factors: the time it takes the tutor to mark written work or organise practical demonstrations; the availability of both tutor and learner to meet; whether or not an assessment needs to be sent away for external verification; the nature of the assessment itself (informal formative assessment of, for example, a class-based activity can be instantaneous, whereas formal formative assessment may require a lengthy marking process). Immediate or near-immediate feedback will be the most useful to the learner. Giving feedback on a written assignment or a practical activity is not effective if it takes place after such a long delay that the learner has begun to forget how they tackled the assessment in the first place. Colleges and awarding bodies often set guidelines about how quickly learners can expect feedback on their work.

5. Feedback should be understood

Above all, feedback needs to be understood by the learner. Having read or listened to feedback, the learner should be able to understand exactly how they have performed in reference to the criteria for the assessment and the course or programme of study. They should be able to describe and then perform the steps necessary for further development, either for the current assessment (if competence has yet to be achieved) or for the next assessment or course. Above all, the learner should be able to make sense of the assessment, and the feedback from it, as a learning episode within the course or programme of study.

Ensuring understanding of feedback is best done in conversation, in a tutorial or other meeting with the learner. This gives the tutor the opportunity to go through the written feedback, and then check understanding with one or two questions. Try to avoid questions that lead to a 'yes' or 'no' answer (often referred to as 'closed-end' questions). Instead, ask an 'open-ended' question that will require the learner to offer a full answer.

An exchange using a closed-end question might go something like this.

Tutor: Do you understand the written feedback, and do you know what you need to do to achieve competence?

Learner: Yes.

An exchange using an open-ended question might go something like this:

Tutor: Tell me what you're going to do in response to the issues raised by the feedback.

Learner: Well, I'll go back to my notes and make sure that I've read them all carefully. Then I'll plan my answer before starting to write, and I'll refer to the course handbook so that I have the criteria for the module in front of me. And when I've finished, I'll read it through carefully and check my spelling as well.

6. Feedback should be delivered in an appropriate environment

The setting in which feedback is given is not always flexible. As teachers and trainers, we may find ourselves giving feedback in all sorts of different places: offices, classrooms, factories, libraries, snack bars or tool sheds. Often, the place where we teach or train is the place where we assess and therefore where we give feedback. This can be an advantage. Giving feedback about how to use a particular piece of milling equipment correctly is a straightforward task if the feedback is being given in the engineering workshop, but rather more difficult if the feedback is being given in a coffee bar. In the same way that we need to use appropriate and realistic resources in our learning and teaching activities, so we may need to employ the same resources when giving feedback (which is, after all, another learning activity in itself).

At other times, a separate environment may be desirable. Giving feedback on a written assignment need not take place in the room where the taught sessions are held: a coffee bar may be preferable if both learner and tutor agree that this more informal atmosphere is appropriate. Other learners may prefer a more quiet and secluded setting, such as the classroom or a staff room. Just as learners may employ preferred learning styles, so they may have a preference for a preferred style of feedback. On other occasions, it may not be possible for the tutor to have any control over where the feedback is given. FE colleges are busy places and teaching accommodation is often at a premium: finding an empty classroom is often a matter of luck. Adult education tutors, working in the community, often have very little control over the kind of accommodation that they teach in and may not be able to gain access to an appropriately quiet space. Sometimes, a venue is available before a class begins and a tutor and a learner can meet before the rest of the group arrives. At other times, more creative thinking may be required to find a suitably confidential space to talk. Some of my more successful tutorials, when working with adults, have been in pubs and clubs where the background noise acts as to mask the conversation being held. Consequently, it may sometimes be necessary to use a location that is far from ideal. In these situations, take the time to check that the learner is comfortable: if not, consider rearranging the tutorial session.

To summarise: if feedback is clear, specific, supportive, timely, understood and delivered in an appropriate environment, then it should encourage learning, help learners make sense of what they need to do next and motivate learners to continue engaging with the learning process.

It's important to remember that no two learners are alike. In this entry from her learning journal, Kim reflects on two very different experiences of giving feedback to learners from the Return–to-Learn group that she teaches on Wednesday afternoons at an outreach centre run by the local FE college. As you read this extract, consider the strengths and weaknesses of Kim's approach during this session.

Bit of a mixed day today, really. One of the group didn't respond at all well to the feedback from the written exercise that they submitted last week, and I ended up having to stay late to sort it all out. There are eight in the group, so I decided to split the session up – we've got three hours after all. I held mini-tutorials for each of them for ten minutes at a time, and then after the coffee break the last hour of the class was spent on our new topic. I was so proud of myself for thinking of doing it like this because this way everybody got to talk to me on a one-to-one basis, and we haven't really had the chance to do that before now. I provided written feedback using the standard college feedback form, and then we went through this form together so that I was sure that each member of the group understood what I had written – I was concerned that they might not all know some of the grammatical terms that I used so I decided to check.

I always arrive early so that I can move the furniture around. This week I did it differently, and I effectively divided the room in half with the tables so that the others could chat or work during the tutorial sessions. When I told the group what we were going to do they all seemed really pleased with the idea.

I had pretty much anticipated how they would all do on the assignment. It was a fairly straightforward exercise: they would pick a story from the news from the last week and write a short report about it. It's an exercise in composition really – spelling, sentence structure and so on. But it was also useful as a comprehension exercise as well – how much they understood from reading the papers about the issue that they chose. Most of them were fine although one – Vicky – needed a lot of correction. So when it was her turn for a tutorial we went through all the things that she needed to do next time and I thought that it all went fine. I remembered to start by giving feedback on what she'd done well before moving on to what she needed to practise. And I'd been really careful to use supportive language and keep it really constructive.

Vicky was a bit quiet during the tutorial and during the coffee break as well, and then it was really hard to get her involved in discussion during the second part of the session. I think that's what made me sit up and take notice – normally she's more than happy to contribute, although she's by no means the most vocal member of the group. She was still a bit upset by the end of the class, and when I was doing my 'Goodbye and see you next time' at the door I had the worst feeling that she might not come back next week. So I asked if she wanted to talk some more about the assignment there and then.

Vicky's behaviour during the class provides Kim with an unambiguous signal: the process of receiving feedback during the mini-tutorial has caused Vicky to withdraw from the group activity. Kim has clearly put a lot of thought into the feedback process, but for Vicky, it has not been successful, and her subsequent behaviour, quite rightly, gave Kim cause for concern.

We ended up staying back for over half an hour! I had to bring it to a close because I had to catch the bus, otherwise it might have lasted even longer. And I needed to tidy the room up before the next group arrived. I couldn't believe how well it went, especially bearing in mind how badly she'd reacted to the initial feedback. By the end of our talk, Vicky was completely back to her usual self

– quite quiet, but definitely determined to do the work that she needed to do for the course. We went over the written feedback again and talked over one or two of the points that I had raised. This second tutorial went really well! Perhaps Vicky just needed more time for the feedback to sink in.

Kim has clearly put a lot of thought into her planning for feedback, and has taken the time to reflect on Vicky's experiences both during the official tutorial, and during the impromptu tutorial that took place after the session. There are several strengths to consider here, but a number of weaknesses to take note of as well.

Kim's feedback session: strengths

Planning for one-to-one feedback
Kim's decision to hold mini-tutorials is a good start: as she herself notes, there have only been limited opportunities for such a discussion before now. And when discussing assessed work, which for adult learners on a Return-to-Learn programme such as this may be posing difficulties, the opportunity for one-to-one feedback helps maintain confidentiality.

Timely feedback
This is a weekly class. Kim collected the assessed work at the previous session, has marked it and written her feedback in time for the next session. This is as fast a turnaround as possible and the learners will appreciate receiving feedback swiftly.

Checking understanding
Kim notes, correctly, that the time spent talking about the written feedback provides a good opportunity to check that each of the learners understands fully what she has written.

Being supportive and constructive
This is always an important issue, of course, but it is often seen as being especially important for adults who have returned to learning after many years away from formal education or training. Courses such as this, held in outreach centres and away from main campuses, are very often designed explicitly to encourage those who would not normally take part – there are many 'widening participation' schemes and policies in operation at the present time. Kim has taken care over how she has worded her feedback, and with good cause: many adult learners cite negative experiences of school – particularly caustic or unkind comments from teachers – as the reason why they stayed away from formal education or training.

Being flexible
As teachers and trainers we do sometimes need to be flexible. Kim's willingness to stay behind (within reason – and it was quite acceptable for Kim to call the extra tutorial to a halt to allow her to catch the bus home) is an example of good practice: learners respond positively to tutors who are willing to go the extra mile for them.

Kim's feedback session: weaknesses

Available time for tutorials
Deciding to have one-to-one meetings with each of the learners is laudable but a cautionary note must be sounded: is ten minutes an acceptable period of time within which to cover all the issues that have been raised by each learner's assessment? Perhaps the plenary activity after the coffee break should have been postponed for a week? This would have allowed

three hours to hold eight tutorials, each of which could have therefore been doubled in length.

Available space for tutorials

Moving the furniture is one of the fundamental rules of adult education and Kim is working hard to make the environment in which she gives feedback as conducive to learning as possible. However, unless her classroom is particularly large, she is running the risk of failing to ensure confidentiality – it may be hard to maintain an air of privacy during each tutorial when the rest of the group are sitting just a short distance away.

Use of language

Kim herself has noted that not all the learners may understand some of the terms that she uses in her feedback. Perhaps she could rewrite the feedback and try to use more everyday language? Or, if certain key expressions or terms do have to be used, she could include a definition within the feedback?

Keeping the learners informed

Kim writes that she told the learners about the tutorials at the start of that session. This may be entirely due to the fact that she only decided to hold tutorials after the end of the previous week's class. It would be good practice to inform the learners of the tutorial process, however, and give them a chance to become used to the idea of a one-to-one conversation with their tutor – which, we must remember, may not necessarily be welcomed by all the members of the group.

THEORY FOCUS **THEORY** FOCUS **THEORY** FOCUS **THEORY** FOCUS **THEORY** FOCUS

Different writers and researchers have looked at the link between feedback and motivation, and often come up with conflicting ideas. One of the themes that appears frequently in research relating to adult students in particular is the importance of encouraging the self-esteem of the student. As teachers and trainers we need to ensure that feedback is not meant to be personal, but as Pat Young (2000) points out, our learners do not always see things in the same light: responses to tutor feedback appear to be influenced more by the learner's self-esteem, rather than their progress or grade, and that such self-esteem issues are particularly acute at the time of the first assessment of the course. James Brown (2007) has added to this argument, concluding from his research that the ways in which learners respond to their marks or grades impacts directly on how they treat and interpret feedback. And he has also argued that learner self-esteem is further affected by the confusion that many learners feel upon reading feedback that lacks specificity, or trying to work out how the number of ticks they may – or may not – have received on their work 'translates' into a grade.

Kim's feedback sessions: alternative techniques

So what could Kim do differently? Perhaps a better question is: what are the alternatives available? There are one or two things that we can consider, although it is important to remember that for Kim, as for any other tutor, actions are often restricted by available time and resources.

Advance notice

By planning the tutorials in advance, and advertising them during the previous week's session, Kim could have organised a timetable for the tutorials. Each learner could have been given a time to attend. This would ensure privacy. Advance notice would also allow learners time to prepare any questions or articulate any concerns of their own.

Longer tutorials

If each tutorial lasted 20 minutes instead of ten, Kim would have had time for a conversation with each learner that could move beyond the assessment and into discussion of the course in more general terms. This would provide Kim with an opportunity to assess informally the general progress of each learner and give the learner more time to ask any questions or raise any issue that he or she had been preparing since the previous week.

Environment

Kim is just one of the tutors who share this classroom in a small outreach centre. If her class had been based at the main college site, it may well have been relatively easy to find a quiet space for the tutorials while the rest of the group chatted and worked. Alternatively, if a quiet space is not available, a busier environment, but one where other members of the learner peer group are not present, could be considered. The busy hubbub of a coffee bar can often help maintain confidentiality during a one-to-one.

Feedback from self-assessment and peer-assessment

We touched on the potential of self- and peer-assessment in Chapters 3 and 5 (you may want to revise those chapters before reading on). The dilemmas relating to self-assessment and peer-assessment are reproduced when considering feedback. To what extent would one learner view feedback given by another learner as valid or reliable? Would the learner simply assume that feedback, like assessment, 'the tutor's job'?

There are ways of making peer feedback work. If feedback is given according to criteria that have been discussed and agreed in advance, it can be a useful tool, as the following journal demonstrates.

CLOSE FOCUS **CLOSE** FOCUS **CLOSE** FOCUS **CLOSE** FOCUS **CLOSE** FOCUS

In this journal extract, John, a lecturer in teacher training, describes his experiences in organising a peer-assessment activity for two groups of teacher-training students – a level 3 PTLLS group, and a level 4 CTLLS group. Some of the issues touch on themes covered in previous chapters.

This week and last have been spent doing the peer seminar presentations with the level 3 group. I decided to get each member of the group to do an individual presentation. I dictated the terms of reference for the presentations and how they would be organised, but I decided to open up the feedback process for debate. I figured that this would achieve two things: first, it would be good revision for the work that we previously did on feedback; second, I thought that it would give the group a greater sense of ownership of the process. The aim of the group discussion was to design a feedback form that could be used for the presentations, and each presentation would get feedback from two other members of the group, chosen at random.

After some discussion, it was decided that the feedback should be delivered in written form under the following headings: communication skills (verbal and non-verbal); content and research; and use of teaching and learning resources. There was also much discussion over a fourth heading, 'relevance', but as the group all teach or train in a range of professional contexts, it was bound to be the case that some of the presentations would be more relevant to some of the peer group than others so this heading was discarded. At the end of the session, all the feedback forms were handed to me, and I made copies of them before handing them out to the relevant learner.

Oral feedback during the sessions was pretty minimal –limited to a few comments such as 'I thought the handout was well-designed' or 'The PowerPoint slides were nice and clear'. I hoped that the written feedback would be a little more insightful, but when reading through them later that day, I was surprised at how anodyne it was. There was a lot of 'I really enjoyed this' or 'Wow! Really great!' in one instance, but no detail about what made that particular presentation so great (an opinion I didn't share). The positive feedback was all quite general, and there was hardly any constructive or developmental feedback at all.

Clearly, the activity has not turned out the way John expected. There is quite a lot to think about here. Does John have unrealistic expectations of his learners? After all, this is a level 3 introductory course, and many of the group may not have experience of assessing through observation. As a relatively new group, there may be an understandable reluctance amongst members to engage in feedback that may be seen as negative or destructive, whereas an experienced teacher would see it as constructive and developmental. Asking the group to discuss the feedback criteria in advance is an excellent idea, but as the group may not have sufficient experience, the peer assessment may lack reliability.

I was unsure at first whether or not to continue with the peer presentations and peer feedback with the level 4 group, but I decided to go ahead. Same set up – negotiated feedback form, random written feedback from two other members of the group. A smaller class size, so we did them all in just the one week. But what a difference! The group as a whole were more comfortable with the entire process, and this came through not only in the session, but also in the written feedback. Some really good points were made during feedback about body language and legibility of slides, and use of jargon was a big topic for debate.

The following week, having had time to go through the written feedback in some detail, I decided to spend some time talking to the level 4 group about how the peer feedback exercise had gone with the other class. I had some ideas regarding why it had been so unsuccessful with the others, but I was interested to get more input. The discussion was really useful, and reinforced what I was thinking. The level 3 learners simply didn't have the experience of giving feedback or of assessing a presentation, and they were nervous.

I had been thinking about two other issues that the group did not come up with. The first one was: did the level 3 learners think that I was simply getting them to do all the work? Did they think that I should have been doing the assessing and the feedback? The second idea was to introduce written self-assessment – I could include on the written feedback form a section where the learner who gave the presentation reflected on what went well and what she or he would change.

There are two other strategies to encourage peer feedback that John could consider.

- **Try a different form of assessment, such as a short-answer quiz like a pub quiz, with the learners divided into small teams. Ask teams to swap answer papers. The informal format of the quiz would prevent it feeling like a formal test, and learners could discuss wrong answers and how they might have been arrived at, and revise key issues relating to right answers as they go along.**
- **Create a model wrong answer containing a mistake that has been made by one or more learners (remembering to keep the mistakes anonymous). Discussing these in class will give learners the**

opportunity to discuss the assessed work, their approaches to it, and their feelings on completing the work and receiving feedback.

Constructing feedback

So what are the guiding principles that we should abide by when constructing feedback? Notwithstanding the variables that we have already discussed, such as environment or timing, it is possible to formulate rules for the construction of feedback that are applicable in all vocational or academic contexts.

- Always start with what went well, before moving on to areas of knowledge or competence that need more work. And always finish on an upbeat note, once again stressing the progress that has been made.
- Avoid the personal. Remember, you are giving feedback on the assessed project, essay or portfolio – not the learner.
- Never compare one learner's performance with another's. The learner's progress should be measured *at all times* against the criteria for the course or programme of study.
- Always include points on which learners can act: feedback only becomes formative when learners can engage with it. Without action points, feedback is reduced to a summary of the learner's current strengths and weaknesses.
- Use a variety of forms of feedback – both oral and written.
- Provide feedback as often as you can.

A SUMMARY OF **KEY POINTS**

In this chapter, we have looked at the following key themes:

> **different reasons for giving feedback as part of the process of assessment;**
> **characteristics of good feedback;**
> **ways of constructing feedback that will support, develop and motivate learners.**

Delivering feedback requires time, space, diplomacy and patience – commodities that are not always available all the time. It is impossible to overestimate the importance of maintaining a regular dialogue with your learners, whether in a formal tutorial, or during the coffee break (an occasion when, as any experienced tutor will tell you, the most worthwhile conversations are held). If your plans for delivering feedback go awry, then the simplest and most important thing is to give the learner the choice: either you can go ahead with your meeting wherever you can find the space, or you can rearrange your meeting for another time.

Branching options

Reflection

Feedback works on many levels. It is quite common, and perfectly understandable, that tutors focus much of their attention on feedback relating to formal, summative assessment. So think about the informal, formative assessment that you carry out, and the feedback that accompanies it, and consider how such informal feedback helps your learners.

Analysis

It is increasingly the case that written feedback is delivered using pre-prepared feedback sheets or templates, normally created by an awarding body or by an education provider.

Consider the forms that you use in your feedback: are they sufficient? Do they differentiate? Would you design them differently? Can you be flexible in terms of how they are used?

Research
How can feedback be conceptualised? Spend some time thinking about the theoretical perspectives that you use to explore learning and teaching, and think about how feedback in all its forms contributes to the learning process.

REFERENCES AND FURTHER READING REFERENCES AND FURTHER READING

Brown, J (2007) Feedback: the student perspective, *Research in Post-compulsory Education* 12(1) pp35-51.

Young, P (2000) 'I Might As Well Give Up: self-esteem and mature learners' feelings about feedback on assignments', *Journal of Further and Higher Education* 24, 3, pp409-418.

7
Recording and tracking assessment information

By the end of this chapter you should:

- **understand the need for keeping, storing and using the information generated by the assessment process;**
- **appreciate the importance of careful record-keeping of assessment results;**
- **be able to distinguish between the different kinds of information relating to assessment, required by different organisations in the learning and skills sector.**

Professional Standards

This chapter relates to the following Professional Standards.

Professional Values

ES5: Working with the systems and quality requirements of the organisation in relation to assessment and monitoring of learner progress.

Professional Knowledge and Understanding

EK5.2: The assessment requirements of individual learning programmes and procedures for conducting and recording internal and/or external assessments.

EK5.3: The necessary/appropriate assessment information to communicate to others who have a legitimate interest in learner achievement.

Professional Practice

EP5.3: Communicate relevant assessment information to those with a legitimate interest in learner achievement, as necessary/appropriate.

PRACTICAL TASK PRACTICAL TASK PRACTICAL TASK PRACTICAL TASK PRACTICAL TASK

Read through the two scenarios that follow. Which situation would you prefer to find yourself in and why?

Scenario one

Imagine that you have taken up your first full-time position at an FE college. You are going to be teaching four different learner groups and each group is working towards a different qualification within the subject area. Two of these groups are on one-year programmes and the other two are on two-year programmes. In total, you have over 50 learners to look after. The academic year is already underway, however: in fact, you will have to take up your new post in January, at the start of the second term in the academic year.

You arrive at your new desk to find a pile of official papers from the examining body responsible for the course, a copy of the assessment criteria for each of the four courses, four registers and seven learner portfolios of evidence – all piled up together.

Looking through all these papers, you realise that you cannot find a list of which learner has completed which assignment, nor any evidence that might help you get to know the learners, and how well they are working and progressing. On speaking to someone else in the staff room, you learn that your predecessor had a tremendous memory, and would always be able to tell you how well any single learner was doing, whether they needed any extra help, and when they handed in their last assignment. But none of this information was ever written down.

Scenario two

Imagine that you have taken up your first full-time position at an FE college. You are going to be teaching five different learner groups and each group is working towards a different qualification within the subject area. One of these groups is on a one-year programme, two are on two-year programmes, and the other two are on two-year part-time programmes. In total, you have over 70 learners to look after. The academic year is already underway, however: in fact, you will have to take up your new post in January, at the start of the second term in the academic year.

You arrive at your new desk to find a series of A4 files stacked up against the wall. Each file is labelled. There are two A4 files for each of the five groups, one labelled 'Tutorial reports' and the other 'Assignment reports'. There is another file labelled 'Awarding Body documents', and a final file labelled 'College assessment procedures'. As you look through these files, you can see which learners have completed assignments, and which have not. It is easy for you to work out when the assignments are due and how they are to be marked. In one of the group files, there are a lot of documents about two particular learners. On closer examination, you realise that this is because these two require extra support in order to carry out their studies.

Having read through the files, you feel that you started to know the learners, even though you have not actually met any of them yet.

Why is all this paperwork necessary?

It is not uncommon for both new and experienced tutors in the Lifelong Learning sector to complain about the amount of form-filling involved in their work. Looking at the piles of feedback forms, course handbooks, assessment criteria and evaluation forms that accumulate during the academic year, it is easy to see why some of us become frustrated. In fact, careful record-keeping is an extremely important part of being a tutor and the different aspects of the role all require a certain amount of record-keeping and form-filling. If this is done on a regular basis, rather than leaving it all to pile up at the end of a course, it need not be a burden. In fact it will make your job, and the jobs of your colleagues, easier.

The real question relating to all the record-keeping and paperwork that both new and experienced tutors have to deal with is: why? For the purposes of this book, we need to focus on the paperwork that accompanies the assessment process in all its guises. Why is it necessary to keep records of every single assignment and every single tutorial? In essence, there are three answers.

1. We need to be able to provide written guidance and feedback to our learners, to accompany the oral feedback that we give in a tutorial or during a class.

2. Records are useful and important to all tutors in helping plan, monitor and review learners' progress. Drawing up a timetable for when assessments are due, and recording the results, helps us remember what we have to do and when. And, of course, keeping written records of learners' progress is a safe and reliable method of monitoring their achievement. Relying solely on memory is inadvisable: no one can remember everything.
3. There are many other organisations and individuals (employers, awarding bodies, admissions tutors) who need to know about the achievements of our learners, for a variety of reasons.

Broadly speaking, we can divide our paperwork processes into two categories: recording progress and recording achievement, although there will always be some overlap between these two. We shall now consider some reasons and useful strategies for keeping records of our learners' assessment activities, using a single case study as an example.

Keeping records to monitor the progress of a group of learners

The majority of courses in the Lifelong Learning sector are assessed in a number of ways. When courses are divided up into components (units or modules being two common terms), there is normally an assessment attached to each component. Remembering who has handed in what, which are late, which need revising before they can be passed and which are still to be completed is far from easy – and if we forget something, or someone, the consequences could be serious. And if we have to do all this remembering for several courses, not just one, then the need for record-keeping becomes obvious.

A simple grid containing a list of learners' names together with a list of the different assignments allows the tutor to see at a glance who has completed the required work and who has yet to do so. Here is an example.

| Learner name | Assignment number, due date and date completed | | | | |
	Unit 1 Due 20/9	Unit 2 Due 22/11	Unit 3 Due 21/2	Unit 4 Due 18/3	Unit 5 Due 20/5
Stenton	20/9	22/11	21/2	18/3	
Poole	20/9	22/11	21/2	18/3	
Powicke	20/9	29/11	28/2		
McKisack	20/9	22/11	21/2	18/3	
Jacob	20/9	22/11	21/2	18/3	
Mackie	20/9	22/11	21/2	18/3	
Black	20/9	22/11	21/2	18/3	
Davies	27/9	13/12			
Clark	20/9	22/11	21/2	18/3	

Let us assume that this tracking grid was last updated on 18 March. A close study of this tracking sheet tells us that seven members of this group are progressing according to schedule. Two of the group, on the other hand, are falling behind in their assessed work. One of these two, Powicke, took an extra week to submit units 2 and 3. A short extension to the due date may not cause any problems (although this will depend on the syllabus). Davies is more of a cause for concern, and after needing extra time to complete units 1 and 2, has yet to submit unit 3, never mind unit 4. There could be several reasons for this. An examination of Davies' individual assessment records would be able to give us more detailed information.

Keeping detailed records to monitor the progress of individual learners

Now that we have set up a way of recording how the group is doing as a whole, we need to think about recording information relating to how individual learners are getting on. Keeping a few notes about each learner's progress, as they work their way through the assignments for the course need not take too long, and will provide a quick point of reference for the tutor. We cannot always remember why an assignment was handed in late or had to be returned for further work. Keeping a few notes will help us track our learners' progress accurately and provide an opportunity to note any concerns that might need to be raised at a subsequent tutorial or with another member of staff.

Assessment Progress Record Learner: *Richard Davies*		
Unit and due date	Date completed	Notes
Unit 1 20/9	27/9	Absent the previous week, so late submission. A bare pass. Handwriting and spelling were both very poor. The task had not been fully understood and comprehension was weak. Refer to feedback form for detail.
Unit 2 22/11	13/12	Intermittent absence led to Richard missing two important sessions relating to the assignment. Similar problems with handwriting and spelling. Comprehension again patchy and task not fully completed when first handed in 6/12. Written feedback given and second submission was enough for a pass.

Our tutor – let's call her Sally – has kept a summary record like this for each of the nine learners in her group in addition to the detailed feedback form that is returned with each assignment after marking (we shall come to this shortly). These summary sheets help her to diagnose quickly how each learner is progressing. The notes that Sally has made here indicate a similar problem with both pieces of written work that Richard has submitted to date and the exact nature of this study problem will need careful consideration. It may be that he needs practice, guidance and supportive feedback from his tutor or it may be that Richard has a specific learning difficulty that has so far been undiagnosed. This happens more frequently than you might think: it is not uncommon for learners to arrive in the post-compulsory sector having gone through compulsory schooling with an undiagnosed learning difficulty, such as dyslexia. This issue is covered in detail in Chapter 9.

Before looking at the detailed feedback form from unit 2, there is one more question to answer. If Sally is teaching and assessing this group of learners, and is in regular contact with them, why does she need to write down all these details when she knows and remembers them anyway? There are several answers to this.

- **It would be a tall order for Sally to remember every detail about all her learners.**
- **If she has an accident or is off sick, or is absent from work for any other reason, it will be a straightforward task for a colleague to pick up where Sally has left off. Without these records, her colleague would be unaware of Richard's difficulties, and this could impact on the provision of developmental feedback or other support.**
- **If Richard does need additional support, the information that Sally has kept on his assessment progress record will be useful.**
- **Record-keeping is an important part of the quality assurance and evaluation processes (discussed in detail in Chapter 8).**

Keeping records of feedback on assessed work so that both tutor and learner can act on that feedback

As we saw in Chapter 6, feedback can be given in different places and at different times. And some forms of feedback are easier to record than others. It is impractical to record informal, formative feedback given during a class while a group of learners is engaged in small-group work. Other forms of formative and summative feedback can usefully be recorded, however. No learner can remember every word of spoken feedback that they receive in a tutorial, or in class, or during any other meeting with their tutor. Some learners will prefer written feedback to oral feedback. A written record will give them something to work with the next time they have to work towards an assignment.

The feedback form that Sally completed after Richard submitted his work for the second time is on page 77. At the start of the form, there is a space for a centre number. This is the unique number that the awarding body gives to each of the colleges that offers its courses. A college will have a different centre number for each of the different awarding bodies. Candidates are sometimes given numbers as well, and it would be this number, rather than the learner's name, that would appear at the top of the feedback form. You will also notice an empty box for the second marker's comments: we shall return to this later on.

This particular feedback form is designed by the awarding body for Sally's course. Sally has to complete one of these feedback forms for each unit assignment completed by each learner. By the end of the course, and assuming that all nine learners submit all five assignments, she will have completed 45 assessment feedback sheets.

The four headings on the feedback form relate to the four assessment criteria that are set out by the awarding body for the course. The marker is invited to comment on each of these four areas and there is space for an action point relating to each of the criteria. Providing constructive points for action is an example of good practice. For feedback to be truly effective, it needs to include specific guidance and developmental comment.

Assessment Feedback Sheet
Candidate Name: Davies, Richard
Centre Number: 12345
Unit Number: 2
Name of first marker: Sally Arnott

Spelling, grammar and use of English
A slight improvement, but you still need to take care over your spelling — there are a lot of spelling mistakes here. Your sentence structure is not improving: you need to make sure that you always write proper sentences. We shall look at some examples of this during our tutorial.

Action Point
Seek extra guidance from me at tutorial, where we shall look at some practice examples. Complete the practice examples before attempting the next unit.

Comprehension
On the whole you have understood the text that was set and your answer demonstrates that you have picked up on most of the key points. Two key issues from the text (wind power and mobile phone masts) were missing from your answer, however. Do make sure that you always read the text carefully before beginning your answer.

Action Point
Look back at the text for unit 2 and find the sections that you missed out. Make a note of these and bring them with you to the tutorial. Talk to me at the tutorial about reading skills.

Structure
Remember what we discussed in class: when structuring your answer, go through each point at a time and finish each one before moving on to the next. At times, you darted between topics and this meant that your answer was a little confusing.

Action Point
Go back to the handout with the model answer that I gave you and complete the exercise that goes with it before our next tutorial. At the tutorial, we will go through your answer.

Evidence of reading and research
You have covered the majority of the issues raised by the set text — well done. There is no evidence of any wider reading, however. We did discuss this in class and I gave out titles of books and websites that might have been useful. A little extra research would help you add detail to your argument. It's also good for you to develop your independent study skills.

Action Point
Let's discuss in our next tutorial how you might address this issue within the next unit.

Comments of second marker

Having marked Richard's submission for unit 2, Sally has written up feedback to include the following action points.

- **She has given Richard some practice exercises for discussion at their next tutorial.**
- **She has asked him to revise the unit 2 assignment.**
- **She will go through the unit at the tutorial and help pinpoint areas for improvement.**
- **She has asked Richard to revise relevant work from a previous class.**

A detailed written feedback report is, in the first instance, for the benefit of the learner. As we have seen in previous chapters, if assessment is to be a learning process, we need to put in place actions that will give our learners the opportunity to develop. Sally has decided on a number of different activities for Richard to carry out before the tutorial, all of which are designed to reinforce learning. These will be assessed at the tutorial and recorded on a tutorial report form. As well as providing Richard with a written record of the agreed action points, this process also provides Sally with a written record of their discussion, which she can use as a basis for discussion at the next tutorial.

Awarding bodies often require tutors to use specific forms when giving feedback on formal, summative assessment, although this will depend on the type of assessment in question: closed exam papers, for example, rarely generate such detailed feedback, whereas assessed presentations or observations will require feedback to be given on an appropriate form. These forms are rarely designed to allow the tutor to write and comment freely: they are divided into different sections relating to the specific criteria for the assignment in question, as in our example above.

A short note on second marking

In order to ensure fairness and consistency when assignments are being marked or graded, it is common practice for a second marker (for whom there is space at the bottom of the feedback form) to look at the assignment. Sometimes, a second marker will look at all the assignments for a course; at other times, just a sample of work will be scrutinised. This is an important part of the evaluation and quality assurance process and is discussed in more detail in Chapter 8.

Tutors frequently come across occasions when they need to design feedback forms of their own (see the example at the end of Chapter 5). This may be because a tutor has decided to set a formative assessment task for a group of learners to complete, or perhaps because the awarding body does not supply a feedback pro-forma. And tutors in adult education are increasingly finding themselves obliged to complete more formal assessment and feedback records, even on recreational and liberal programmes. Some tutors design and use feedback sheets in addition to those provided by an awarding body, although it is good practice to check with the awarding body that this is acceptable practice (normally through contacting the external verifier or external examiner, the person who acts as liaison between the college and the awarding body).

The design of such forms can vary. The form can be divided into sections, one for each of the assessment criteria, or be unstructured, so that it does not influence the way in which the feedback is laid out. The tutor can then go through points as he or she wishes. It may be desirable to create a checklist, where the tutor can tick off each of the criteria as the learner achieves them. The exact layout is a matter of choice, or perhaps taste: if you are using your own feedback form, it would make sense to design a form that both you and your learners find easy to follow and to understand.

Keeping records of tutorial feedback and assessment to support the developmental process

While they are not a feature of every course or programme of study in the Lifelong Learning sector tutorials (one-to-one meetings between tutors and learners) are an important part of the teaching and learning process – and therefore of the assessment process as well. How can the issues discussed at the tutorial – concerns that the learner or the tutor may have about progress and assessment – be recorded and acted on?

Up to this point, Sally has used a group tracking grid and an individual summary sheet for each learner. She designed both of these herself. She has also completed a pro-forma individual feedback form for each unit assignment submitted so far. For the tutorial, she will complete a written report. Sally can record Richard's progress since he submitted his unit 2 assignment and offer further developmental feedback. The awarding body does not provide a tutorial report form for Sally to complete. In this case, the paperwork is designed and monitored by the college where Sally works. This is common practice in the sector: it helps to maintain consistency between different tutors within the same programme of study, and between different curriculum areas.

From the report form on page 80, we can see that during the tutorial Richard and Sally have focused on three areas of Richard's progress and that four courses of action have been decided. Importantly, the space for further comments allows Sally to note two other things. First, Richard is still motivated and wishes to continue with his studies. Second, Richard is himself aware that he may need extra support (of some kind) and is receptive to this.

PRACTICAL TASK PRACTICAL TASK PRACTICAL TASK PRACTICAL TASK PRACTICAL TASK

1. From the documentation relating to Richard, what do you think the causes of his difficulties might be? Note the different issues raised by this case study and make a note of the different actions that Sally has taken in response to each of these issues.

2. So far, Sally has been using forms designed by herself, by the awarding body for her course, and by the college where she works. Where would you look for relevant forms and records for the subject area in which you teach? You could speak to your mentor about this or, if you are already teaching in a college (either in employment or on placement), you could ask a colleague who works in the same subject area.

These two questions may seem to be worlds apart but in fact each is as important as the other for a tutor. As teachers and trainers we need to be aware of any difficulties that our learners may have. In this case study, Sally's evaluation of Richard's progress has led to her realising that he needs some extra support. This will require the involvement of another member of staff – a learning support assistant – but there are other learning activities that Sally can plan herself, such as the additional formative assessment exercises (action point 2) and a follow-up tutorial (action point 3).

Such well-planned assessment for learning, following on from a careful process of monitoring and evaluation, would quickly collapse if Sally had to be away from college and there

---

Lakeside College of Further Education Tutorial Report Form

Learner: Richard Davies   **Tutor:** Sally Arnott
Course: Access to English   **Date:** 5/1

Issues brought forward from last tutorial

Not applicable: this is our first tutorial.

Issues raised during tutorial

1. Richard needs to ensure that he catches up with work that he misses due to absence. Some of the problems that he encountered with unit 2 were due to having missed relevant exercises in class and not completing them on his return.
2. Richard needs to keep up to date with weekly assessment tasks – these will help when unit assignments come due.
3. Spelling and grammar continue to cause problems. In tutorial, Richard told me that he has always found this difficult and that he always felt that this was one of the reasons why he didn't enjoy school.

Action points arising from tutorial

1. Richard will work to improve his attendance record.
2. Richard will work through a series of smaller test exercises before the unit 3 assignment.
3. We will have another tutorial in four weeks' time to go through the test exercises and discuss classroom progress.
4. Sally will make an appointment for Richard with the Learning Support office.

Further comments

Richard is keen to continue his programme of study and is aware that his language and literacy skills need developing. He is happy just to practise but we decided between us that some extra Learning Support would be beneficial. Richard is comfortable with this, as we have a Learning Support worker in our group anyway, helping another member of the class.

---

was no record of what she had done. And Richard will undoubtedly benefit from having a written action plan. By following a sequence of actions that are recorded and prompted in the documents and forms that Sally completes as she works, she can be sure of having taken all the steps necessary to obtain the support that Richard needs. Because all the other tutors in Sally's college follow the same procedure – as they follow the same process of recording what happens – any learner who was experiencing difficulty would receive the same guidance and advice.

Recording any additional support required by one or more learners

In Chapter 9 we will look at the facilities available that allow learners facing particular difficulties or disabilities to participate in education and training. Normally, a provider would have a section or department dedicated to co-ordinating and providing the extra support that a learner with dyslexia or a wheelchair user might need: this is often referred to as learning support. Sometimes a learner will receive help on a regular basis from appropriately qualified specialists, for example, a note-taker or a sign-language interpreter. At other times, a learner may require specialist equipment, rather than specialist help, in order to participate.

It is increasingly the case that many programmes of study can adapt assessment methods in order to allow learners with disabilities to take part. Normally it is the awarding body that makes the decision and relevant information has to be forwarded to them. Once again, therefore, the information kept by the tutor would be used to help ascertain the assessment needs of a particular learner.

Recording end-of-course achievement for accreditation

When the course comes to an end, Sally will need to let the awarding body know which of her learners have successfully completed their studies and which have yet to do so. And of course, other tutors teaching the same course throughout the country will also be sending in their results. If we take into consideration the number of different courses on offer in further and adult education, it is not too hard to appreciate how many sets of results need to be submitted. Awarding bodies and examining bodies work with colleges on a regular basis throughout the year, not just at the year end, and this relationship is explored in detail in Chapter 8. For the moment, we need to concentrate on how those results are collected and submitted in time for certificates, diplomas and other awards to be given.

Final results from courses can be collected from a number of different assessment activities: courses are often divided into units or modules, each of which has its own assessment. As well as finding different kinds of assessment at different times, it is also common practice for different people to be involved in marking them. Examination papers, for example, are often sent away to be graded by an external marker. Coursework-based assignments are normally marked internally, with perhaps a sample being sent away for checking (see Chapter 8). Several tutors may be teaching specific units within a larger programme, and each tutor will be responsible for assessment for that one unit. And it would of course be very difficult for a practical assignment based on observation to be carried out by anyone other than a tutor at the institution where the learner was based. As Sally is the lead tutor for her course, it is her responsibility to collect all the results together at the end of the programme and submit them to the examining body. Normally, this process involves completing a results form sent out by the awarding body for this purpose. Once told by Sally which learners have successfully completed the assignments, the awarding body can issue them with their certificates.

The timing of these actions varies between programmes. Candidates who are working towards an NVQ within the workplace are able to begin and end their studies at any time in the year: they are not restricted to starting study when the new academic year begins in September. Other courses may have an assessment timetable that has to be strictly adhered to: if the learners (or the tutor) miss the deadline, awards may not be given. As lead tutor,

Sally has the responsibility of finding out when the assignments are due, when the results need to be submitted, which forms need to be completed, and what information is needed on them.

Recording achievement for the purpose of quality assurance and evaluation

It is important to make sure that assessment procedures are carried out fairly and consistently within the different departments or curriculum areas of an FE college or adult education provider. And it is equally important to make sure that assessment procedures are carried out fairly and consistently between different education and training establishments across the country. These important quality assurance issues are discussed in detail in Chapter 8. Tutors' records form an important body of evidence for these processes of checking and second-checking.

Keeping records: hints and tips

Here are six practical steps and strategies that you may find useful.

1. Ask for help

If you are unsure how to complete a form correctly, ask someone else for help. A more experienced tutor, or a mentor, will not mind spending a few minutes with you if you are unsure about the correct way to complete a particular form. Often, an awarding body will provide examples of completed forms. It may also be useful to ask a colleague for examples of forms from previous terms or academic years. The easiest way to learn how to carry out a task is very often to see an example of the finished product.

2. Work out a method for keeping records and stick to it

Spending a little time on sorting and filing records will make your life much easier at the end of the year, or when it is time for course evaluation and quality assurance. Your records will often need to be checked by other departments within your college, as well as by external agencies such as awarding bodies or the Office for Standards in Education, Children's Services and Skills (Ofsted). These procedures will go more smoothly if your records are clearly labelled and easy to consult.

3. Read the instructions carefully

Many forms need to be reproduced and extra copies sent to other departments or organisations. The difference between two different forms may only be slight but a mix-up could cause all kinds of bureaucratic problems. Some forms may need to be sent off within a specified time. Make sure that you fill in the right forms at the right time and keep a copy for your own records.

4. Use a computer

You do not need to be a technical wizard to use a computer for storing feedback forms. Using a computer to store records takes up less space than a number of box files; using a computer for feedback allows what you write to be enlarged easily – your learners will not have to decipher your handwriting; you can email feedback to learners (this is particularly useful for part-time learners who may attend college only once a week). The important thing to remember is: always save a back-up copy of everything that you do.

5. Keep up-to-date

It is not always easy to set aside a regular time in the working week to settle down to complete your paperwork but if you can keep to some kind of timetable it will make life easier. It is all too easy to lose or forget something, so if you have papers to store in different files, keep them all safe in a 'to do' folder.

6. Think about what you write

The kinds of records and forms that we have been looking at are invariably in the public domain. That is to say, lots of different people (learners, staff, people who work for other educational organisations) are entitled to read them. Everything that you record should be reasonable, fair and justifiable.

PRACTICAL TASK PRACTICAL TASK **PRACTICAL TASK** PRACTICAL TASK **PRACTICAL TASK**

Spend a few minutes writing a list of all the different forms and documents that you have encountered as a learner on your teacher-training course. Focus on the records that relate to assessment. What happens to these forms? Who reads them? What use is made of them?

A SUMMARY OF **KEY POINTS**

In this chapter, we have looked at the following key themes:
> **reasons for keeping records relating to learners' progress in formative and summative assessment;**
> **ways of constructing and accessing appropriate forms;**
> **strategies for keeping records up-to-date and easily navigable.**

The role of the tutor, when assessing learners, is not simply restricted to the business of assessing learning. A successful assessment procedure also involves the recording, storing and circulation of results, feedback and any other pertinent information for potentially several different interested parties. At times, it may feel like a chore and it is highly unlikely to be one of the reasons why you want to become a teacher, but record-keeping is an important part of the everyday life of people working in education and training and it is worth taking the time to get it right.

Branching options

Reflection

It has been known for tutors to complain occasionally about the amount of paperwork that they have to do. There are plenty of anecdotes to suggest that the paperwork burden has increased for tutors throughout the Lifelong Learning sector. As you look through the paperwork that surrounds the assessment processes in your curriculum or organisation, think about what happens to it. Who will read it, and why do they need to know about it?

Analysis

Take a step back from the form-filling that you have to do on a regular basis, and think about how it shapes your working life. Does the fact that some tasks are accompanied and shaped by paperwork mean that other things get left undone? Or, to put it another way, which kinds of activities are privileged or made more important by paperwork, and what kinds of things might get lost sight of?

Research

The proliferation of paperwork can be interpreted as an aspect of the managerialist, audit cultures within which we work. Using the suggestions for further reading below, research and reflect on this aspect of the tutor's professional life.

REFERENCES AND FURTHER READING REFERENCES AND FURTHER READING

Lea, J, Hayes, D, Armitage, A, Lomas, L and Markless, S (2003) *Working in Post-Compulsory Education*. Maidenhead: Open University Press.

Strathern, M (ed) (2000) *Audit Cultures: anthropological studies in accountability, ethics and the academy*. London: Routledge.

Tummons, J (2010) *Becoming a Professional Tutor in the Lifelong Learning Sector*. Second edition. Exeter: Learning Matters.

8
Evaluation

By the end of this chapter you should:

- **understand the need for evaluation of the assessment process;**
- **be able to describe a range of strategies to support and encourage evaluation;**
- **understand the relevance of the quality assurance policies of different stakeholders in the learning and skills sector to the evaluation process.**

Professional Standards

This chapter relates to the following Professional Standards.

Professional Values

ES5: Working with the systems and quality requirements of the organisation in relation to assessment and monitoring of learner progress.

Professional Knowledge and Understanding

EK5.1: The role of assessment and associated organisational procedures in relation to the quality cycle.

Professional Practice

EP5.1: Contribute to the organisation's quality cycle by producing accurate and standardised assessment information, and keeping appropriate records of assessment decisions and learners' progress.

EP5.2: Conduct and record assessments which adhere to the particular requirements of individual learning programmes and, where appropriate, external bodies.

What is evaluation?

In the past, when I handed out end-of-term questionnaires to learners, I often met with less than enthusiastic responses to my request for them to be filled in. On some occasions, I asked learners to bring them back the following week, but some always forgot. On other occasions, I asked learners to complete the questionnaire there and then, or during a coffee break, in order to make sure that as many questionnaires as possible were returned. But I still encountered resistance. Learners complained that form-filling took up valuable time when they could be learning and studying. When they asked why the questionnaires were necessary, I would say: 'They help me work out how well the course is going, how well you are learning and how well I am teaching'. And in a nutshell, that is the main purpose of evaluation: to see whether the thing that we are evaluating is fit for the purpose for which it has been designed. Evaluation is an important aspect of any education or training provision. Evaluation can be carried out at different times, in different ways and for different audiences.

If you are currently studying for a teaching qualification, or have recently finished a teacher-training course, your course will have been evaluated in several ways and you will have been involved in the process at some point. How is your course evaluated, when was it evaluated and why do you think this process is important?

As teachers and trainers, we will encounter evaluation at many stages of our professional life. Evaluation can be carried out in many different ways and for different reasons. It is outside the scope of this book to explore educational evaluation in depth but a brief summary of the issues that evaluation seeks to address includes the following.

- **Were the learners and teachers satisfied with the programme?**
- **Were other stakeholders, such as employers or funding bodies, satisfied with the programme?**
- **Did the programme provide value for money?**
- **Did the programme recruit sufficiently and did all the learners remain on the course and complete their studies successfully?**
- **Should the programme be run differently next time?**

As it is an integral part of any educational programme, assessment has to be evaluated just like the other aspects of the programme. How should this be done and who, apart from tutors and learners, should be involved in the process?

Why evaluate assessment?

Evaluation of education and training is sometimes taken for granted. Among the questionnaires, meetings or Ofsted inspections (three very different evaluation tools, to which we shall return later) it can be all too easy to forget why evaluation is necessary. Evaluation of assessment is all about judging the extent to which the assessment does what it is supposed to do. It is all well and good for the tutor to say 'This assessment will test the extent to which the learners can use precision measuring equipment', but we still need to answer the question: 'How do you, the tutor, know that the assessment *will* test the extent to which the learners can use precision measuring equipment?'

In earlier chapters, we have explored a wide range of issues relating to assessment. If an assessment activity has been properly planned and carried out, it must have certain characteristics. It must be valid and reliable (Chapter 4) and have proper feedback procedures in place (Chapter 6). Here is a checklist of questions that we need to ask when evaluating any assessment process.

Checklist for the evaluation of the assessment process

Was the assessment:

- **valid and reliable?**
- **authentic and sufficient?**
- **marked or graded fairly?**
- **easily understood by the learners?**
- **accompanied by sufficient feedback?**
- **recorded using the correct documentation?**

In this extract from his learning journal, Gwilym, a trainee teacher currently on placement at an FE college, reflects on a short test that he devised and the feedback he received from Sarah, his mentor.

My mentor suggested that I set up a formative test for the BTEC group, which has been brilliant – really good experience. She helped me on a couple of occasions when I knew what I wanted to ask but wasn't sure how to word the question and I wrote the rest myself. So the group did the test and they seemed pretty happy – no grumbles during the session, which was good. Later the same day I was in the staff lounge marking the papers and writing up my feedback when Sarah came in and asked me how I'd got on. I told her about the session and how it had gone quite smoothly and I asked if she'd mind looking at the feedback I'd been writing so far – I was about halfway through. She spent a few minutes flipping through the papers and then gave them back to me and said that I should look at which questions people had made mistakes on.

By the time I'd marked them all, I realised that out of fourteen people in the group, ten of them had got the same question wrong. I pointed this out to Sarah, who asked me to pass her a copy of the test paper. She read through the paper once more and asked me to think again about question 7 (the one that caused all the problems). I didn't realise until Sarah pointed it out that it was based on a topic that we wouldn't be covering until the next unit! It seems obvious now, but it was a silly mistake. Good job it was only a class test and not an end of term exam.

Having evaluated the test paper, Gwilym and Sarah have found the problem: Gwilym had set a question that related to a subject that had not yet been covered in class. The test was not valid. This discovery may have been made during an informal chat in the staff lounge but it is still a good example of evaluation at work. The assessment itself is flawed and needs to be redesigned. Evaluation has highlighted a weakness in the assessment process.

It is also desirable to evaluate the assessment product – that is to say, the assessed work produced by the learners. Tutors can learn a lot from a careful scrutiny of assessed work. This second learning journal extract is from Jaswant, a new tutor in numeracy and literacy, who looks back at the experiences of a group of learners tackling a particular numeracy assignment. Jaswant teaches on a part-time basis and is studying for her teaching qualification at the same time, also on a part-time basis.

We were looking at some fairly straightforward arithmetic this week, so I thought I'd finish with a short test. I didn't want it to be really formal, because I was worried about putting people off or putting them on the spot, so I designed a quiz that they could do in teams, like a television programme. We'd been studying assessment in teacher-training, so I was really careful to make sure that I only asked questions about stuff we'd done and I spent ages reading and rereading the questions so it was easy to understand. It was good to be able to put into practice some of the ideas that I'd covered as a learner.

After the quiz, the teams swapped papers and we marked them in class. The tone was just right and there was a good deal of pride when the answer was the right one. When someone had made a mistake, we went through the answer on the whiteboard to show the working out. What made me jump was that there was one question, on decimals, that all four teams got wrong and they all got the same wrong answer. We went through the correct answer and then I asked them to say, one at a time, what they'd done. And they'd all done the same thing – they'd all made the same mistake. So I stopped the feedback session and put the question back on the board. One at a time, I asked each team to explain how they'd set about solving it. But I never got the chance to hear all the workings out in full, because as the first team said what they'd done, the others were all agreeing, saying that they'd done the same because I'd told them to. I was totally nonplussed – didn't have a clue what to say for a minute or two. So I said that I'd go back over it, during the break. We finished the answers, and off they went.

During coffee, I went back to my notes and my plan for the session where we covered decimals. The only thing I could think of was that I had made a mistake on the day, or hadn't explained something as clearly as I needed to. I checked all my notes, and my transparencies, and they seemed fine. So when the learners came back after coffee, I asked them if they'd mind going over it one more time. And as we went through the different stages of the arithmetic, it came to me where the mistake must have come. I'd told them a shortcut method for working out where decimal points should go, and that's where the mistake came. They'd all concentrated on the shortcut rather than the proper method and come unstuck.

Jaswant's evaluation of the assessment – which effectively took place during the session – has highlighted a different issue. The fact that all the learners made the same mistake in a test that was valid and reliable made Jaswant think in broader terms about why everyone had made the same mistake. The evidence of the learners' actual work during the quiz helped her to spot the problem, which was not to be found in the assessment process itself, but in her teaching of one of the sessions prior to the quiz. The evaluation of the product of assessment – the actual answers given by the learners – can serve a number of purposes.

Checklist for the evaluation of the assessment product

What does the work done by the candidates tell us about:

- **what they have and have not learned?**
- **how they have been taught?**
- **the extent to which they have understood the questions that they have been asked?**

The questions that we have raised about the evaluation of assessment procedures and products are not mutually exclusive. Evaluating the extent to which an assessment activity has successfully measured and recorded learning can be carried out using a variety of approaches. In the second of our case studies, Jaswant's analysis of her learners' work – and, specifically, the common mistake that they all made – led her to reflect on and question her own teaching strategies. Her planned assessment activity was sound. In our first case study, Gwilym's analysis of the answers produced by his learners led to the conclusion that the assessment instrument itself was invalid. Gwilym's teaching was not a concern: the mistake lay in the fact that the test asked a question based on an aspect of course content that had not yet been covered by the group.

Formal evaluation procedures and processes

So far, we have seen two examples of informal evaluation. 'Informal' makes a distinction between the kind of evaluation that tutors need to build into everyday assessment practice (a conversation with a colleague, or a moment of quiet reflection are two effective methods of achieving this) and the kind of evaluation that involves official meetings, policy statements and representatives of other organisations. By definition, informal evaluation is sporadic and unpredictable: not all tutors are as reflective as Jaswant, or as fortunate as Gwilym in having a sharp-eyed mentor. Relying on teachers and trainers to evaluate assessment activities on an 'as-and-when' basis is simply inadequate. If formal evaluation procedures are in place, we can ensure that evaluation takes place in all colleges, across all departments. Gwilym and Jaswant were evaluating a formative assessment activity that they had designed themselves. What would happen if similar problems of validity and reliability were found in summative assessments that were being completed by learners from colleges across the country? All the issues raised in these two checklists are applicable to evaluation in formal and informal contexts. Now let's look at the formal context.

Maintaining standards

It is likely that more than one tutor will be involved in the teaching and assessing of a course or programme of study during the academic year. Tutors may deliver part or all of a programme, depending on knowledge and experience, and may be present at college on either a full-time or part-time basis. Several different tutors may be involved in the delivery and assessment of a single programme of study. In cases such as this, the need to maintain consistency among a group of several tutors is obvious.

Hoping to bump into each other during a coffee break and discuss their current assessment problems is not a recipe for thorough evaluation: teachers and trainers are busy people with many demands on their time. So it makes sense for colleges and teams of teachers within them to organise formal opportunities for evaluation. 'Team meetings' or 'programme meetings' like these provide a valuable opportunity for tutors within a specific programme area to discuss problems – and potential solutions – relating to a range of issues, including assessment. Here are some of the assessment issues that a team meeting might look at.

Creating and using formative assessments

Having spent time constructing formative assessment tasks for our learners, it would seem sensible to discuss and share these strategies with other tutors in our team. Tutors have preferred styles of teaching, as we have discussed, and this often spills over into assessment practice as well. By discussing our ideas and strategies with other tutors, we can expand our own repertoire and pick up ideas, strategies or resources that we can use in the future.

Discussing the interpretation and implementation of summative assessments

When a new syllabus is published, it is the responsibility of the tutors to acquaint themselves with all the material relating to the unit or programme in question. This will include assessment issues such as methodologies, marking schemes, criteria and timings. Normally, the dissemination of guidance and information about these new assessment guidelines would be the responsibility of a head of department or another, similar senior member of the teaching staff, such as a programme leader, pathway leader or lead tutor.

Comparing marking and grading within the institution (second marking or internal moderation)

In order to ensure reliability (see Chapter 4), it is important to maintain consistency in marking and grading. One of the ways in which reliability is maintained is through the use of explicit criteria and marking procedures, set down by awarding bodies for summative assessment purposes. Nationally applied standards help maintain standards between institutions as well as within them. The first stage in this process is to ensure that marking or grading standards are being applied consistently within a programme team. Moderation is an important process that can take place at different times in the academic year, depending on the programme in question. For some qualifications, regular moderation meetings will be held. For other qualifications, moderation will happen as it is needed. Sometimes, all learner work will need to be moderated; at other times, only a sample of work will be reviewed.

CLOSE FOCUS **CLOSE** FOCUS **CLOSE** FOCUS **CLOSE** FOCUS **CLOSE** FOCUS

Second marking can be carried out in two ways:

- **with sight of the first marker's grades and feedback on the learner's work;**
- **without seeing the first marker's grades and comments – this is often referred to as 'blind' second marking.**

The theory behind blind second marking is that it prevents the second marker from being swayed by any comments that the first marker has made, further increasing reliability.

Comparing assessment procedures within an institution

To ensure reliability, we also need to ensure that the procedures and policies relating to assessment are carried out fairly and consistently. If two groups of learners are studying for the same award, the reliability of their assessment can hardly be guaranteed if one of the groups has been given more time and resources to complete their assignments than the other. It is the responsibility of a named member of the teaching staff to check that processes and procedures are applied consistently and provide feedback to the awarding body in question. This can be done by the programme leader. For some qualifications, awarding bodies insist on the appointment of an internal verifier, who will need to hold a specialist qualification.

A note on terminology

The terms 'moderation' and 'verification' are used in different contexts by various awarding bodies and by writers and researchers. I have used moderation in reference to comparing and checking the marking and grading of assessment, and verification in reference to comparing and checking assessment procedures. A worthwhile exercise would be to find out which terms are used within your curriculum area. City and Guilds, for example, use internal verifiers for both functions.

Maintaining standards

It is now time to think about the bigger picture and to look at the further education sector as a whole. The large number of qualifications and awards offered in the Lifelong Learning sector are regulated by a number of different regional and national organisations. For now, we shall focus on the ways in which moderation and verification issues are managed between institutions, before going on to look at the many different organisations, or stakeholders, who have an interest or involvement in the assessment process.

Comparing marking and grading

Just as the internal moderator works to ensure reliability among teachers and trainers within an institution, so the external moderator (also sometimes called the external examiner) works to ensure reliability between providers. The external moderator is normally appointed by, and accountable to, the awarding body and his or her role is to ensure that marking and grading criteria are being consistently applied between different institutions. Because they are not employed by the providers in question, they are seen as unbiased and impartial and their prime responsibility is to the awarding body. An external moderator will frequently have responsibility for a number of institutions, usually within a particular geographic area. Once the external moderation process has been carried out (generally at fixed points in the academic year) the external moderators will meet to discuss and evaluate their work.

Ensuring adherence to nationally-defined procedures and policies

It is the external verifier's job to ensure that procedures and policies for assessment are carried out consistently in different places. The consistent application of procedures and criteria is a condition that a provider must meet in order to continue offering a particular programme of study: if an external verifier decides that a provider is not running a programme properly, the awarding body may remove their right to offer the award. At the other end of the scale, if another provider wants to run an existing programme of study for the first time, the external verifier will be responsible for giving approval, a process known as validation. The role of external moderator and external verifier is sometimes combined, with one individual taking on all these responsibilities: it depends on the awarding body in question. The external verifier takes the results of the verification and moderation processes and circulates them to the wider world.

There are several other organisations and groups in addition to colleges, adult education providers, private training companies and examining bodies who are interested in how well assessment is carried out – that is, not only the results of assessment, but also the evaluation of assessment.

PRACTICAL TASK PRACTICAL TASK **PRACTICAL TASK** PRACTICAL TASK **PRACTICAL TASK**

Before reading on, make a list of the different individuals or organisations that you think have an interest in you as a learner on a teacher-training course. As you make your list, write down the reasons why you think these different stakeholders are involved.

Stakeholders in the evaluation of assessment process

Teachers and trainers

As a tutor, it is always nice to know when you are doing something right. The opportunity to swap notes with other tutors is a great practical help, particularly to new practitioners for whom assessment and grading processes and procedures may be unfamiliar. Receiving feedback from the moderation process at any stage (either internally or externally) can be a great help to new tutors who may lack confidence in their judgement. When a second marker or an external examiner agrees with marking decisions and says that feedback was helpful and supportive to the learners, it boosts a new tutor's confidence. Being involved in moderation is also important as a form of broader professional development: it allows tutors from different colleges, who might not otherwise have the opportunity to talk, to come together and reflect on assessment and evaluation practice. Moderation meetings offer new teachers and trainers a good opportunity to develop. When attending these meetings (which are often chaired by an internal verifier or course or programme leader) a new tutor can see samples of learners' work that have already been marked, and talk to more experienced tutors about how they approach the process of assessment.

The evaluation process can also help teachers and trainers in their relationship with their learners. It is not easy to tell a learner that they have failed an assignment or a course, or that they still have a lot more work to do before their portfolio of evidence can be said to demonstrate competence. The confidence that evaluation can provide on a personal level, together with knowing that the evaluation process is fair and impartial, can help make this process less problematic. The tutor can be confident in his or her judgement and the learner will know that the decision is a fair one.

Learners

Learners need to have confidence in every aspect of their educational journey, that they are being treated fairly and consistently, that they will have all the resources that they need to complete their courses, and that their qualifications and awards are worth the paper they are written on. If learners lack confidence in the quality of the educational award that they are studying for, they may lose motivation.

Awarding bodies are aware of the importance of involving learners in the different parts of the programme. When an external verifier visits an educational establishment, he or she will make a point of not only moderating learner work and checking that the correct procedures are all in place, but also of meeting and talking to learners who are currently working towards the award in question. Involving learners in the evaluation process can help to generate a sense of ownership of the process, aiding motivation and achievement. Involvement also demonstrates the transparency of the evaluation process, and increases learner confidence in it.

Awarding bodies

Awarding bodies need to know that their programmes of study are being properly installed and managed across the country. It is important for them to maintain the quality, the credibility and the profitability of their qualifications. Through validation (see above), revalidation (where an institution is revisited by the awarding body to check that the standards, policies and procedures for the programme are still being upheld), moderation and verification, awarding bodies can guarantee that their programme of study is being delivered to the highest standards.

Trade and industry bodies

Many of the qualifications and awards that are offered in the Learning and Skills sector are designed to meet the needs of specific sectors of industry. Sector Skills Councils and other bodies that represent different industry sectors play an important role in the creation and maintenance of qualifications, drawing up national occupational standards (which qualifications will need to address), and developing programmes of education and training such as apprenticeships, and foundation degrees. Trade and industry have an important role to play in defining criteria for a wide range of vocational and technical awards and qualifications that will ensure that learners studying for an award are actually acquiring the skills and competences that different trade and industry sectors require.

Employers

An employer is not necessarily seeking candidates with specific vocational qualifications. There will be times when a position is only open to candidates who hold particular industry-regulated qualifications but there will be other times when an employer will base a decision to employ someone on the broader qualifications that they hold. Employers may be looking for candidates with transferable skills or who show the potential to benefit from further in-house training. Once again, the prime issue is of confidence: an employer needs to be certain that a specific qualification demonstrates a specific level of attainment, and it is the evaluation process that ensures that confidence.

Other educational establishments

For many learners, one programme of study will lead to another. On other occasions personal circumstances, such as moving house, may force a learner to transfer to a different educational establishment. By being able to guarantee the quality of all the different qualifications that are available in the post-compulsory sector, other colleges and universities can instantly build up a profile of any learner who is seeking to enrol on a course with them.

Parents and guardians

Just because we work in post-compulsory education, it does not mean that parents no longer maintain an interest: the investment in time, the contributions towards course fees and other financial aid, and broader support at home all lead to many parents and guardians continuing to take an active interest in the progress of the young adults for whom they are responsible.

Funding bodies

Every year, several billions of pounds are spent on education and training provision across FE colleges, work-based training providers, adult education centres and such like. With such large sums of public money involved, it is hardly surprising that demands for accountability are high. There are two distinct organisations involved in funding the Lifelong Learning sector, both of which were established relatively recently following the demise of the Learning and Skills Council. The Skills Funding Agency (SFA) is responsible for the training of adults, and has a specific remit to manage National Apprenticeships. The Young People's Learning Agency (YPLA) works in conjunction with local education authorities (who provide the actual funding) to manage education and training opportunities for people aged 16-18.

Other external agencies

There are other organisations that have a role in assuring the quality of education and training provided, and therefore have a direct interest in the assessment of learners.

Perhaps the best known such organisation is Ofsted, which even amongst the very newest entrants to the education and training workplace, needs little introduction. Ofsted was originally established to inspect the quality of provision in schools. Its remit was expanded in 2000 by the Lifelong Learning Act, which brought about a collaboration with the Adult Learning Inspectorate (ALI – now defunct). In April 2007, Ofsted and the ALI merged to create one inspectorate. Ofsted is now responsible for the inspection of all provision in the post-compulsory sector (colleges, work-based provision, community education, prison education) and for the inspection of teacher training for the Lifelong Learning sector, although its remit also includes childcare provision, fostering and adoption agencies as well as state-maintained schools.

Clearly, there are a great many parties who are interested in education in general terms, and in assessment and evaluation. Thanks to the use of a range of different evaluation methods, these stakeholders can obtain the information that they need in order to justify and continue their engagement with the processes and products of assessment. Here is a summary of evaluation methods, together with some further evaluation methodologies that have been mentioned.

A summary of evaluation methods and practices relating to assessment

- **Internal and external moderation and verification**
  By checking each other's marking, we can spot discrepancies and obtain support for our own assessment decisions. Refer back to Gwilym's case study for an example.
- **Validation**
  Awarding bodies can set and monitor strict criteria for every college that offers one of its qualifications.
- **External inspection**
  Ofsted is an ever-present aspect of life in further education.
- **Using performance indicators**
  Statistical analysis can be revealing. For example, a sudden drop in the number of learners achieving a particular qualification, when the statistics for the other courses being offered all show an increase in pass-rates, may indicate a problem relating to the assessment for that qualification.
- **Gauging learners' responses to assessment (through end-of-term questionnaires, or meetings with external verifiers)**
  It is important to provide a range of opportunities for learners to give feedback on their experiences of learning, including assessment.
- **College-based observations of teaching**
  It is common practice for tutors to observe their peers, and for line managers to observe members of their teaching teams, on a regular basis. This is still an issue that causes debate, if not controversy. Class-based assessment practice may well form a beneficial focus of inspection in this manner.
- **Staff-learner committees**
  Staff-learner committees provide valuable opportunities for feedback from the learners that go beyond an end-of-term questionnaire. Again, assessment practice may be an issue of discussion at such a meeting.
- **College self-assessment reports (SAR)**
  Following the Ofsted template, it is now common practice for colleges to compile self-assessment reports on an annual basis. This college-wide process of evaluation is normally used to identify current areas of good practice and areas that require improvement. Assessment of learning may be an area for concern in an SAR.
- **Reflective practice**
  Reflective practice is a key theme in post-compulsory education and training. By stepping back from our teaching and critically examining what we do and why we do things the way we do, we can evaluate our own assessment practice,and be constantly aware of the potential to improve on what we currently do. Refer back to Jaswant's case study for an example.

Evaluation and the part-time tutor

Part-time tutors work in may different capacities, and it is unsurprising that their exposure to evaluation regimes is similarly variable. Part-time tutors working for a large college, for example, will often have to adhere to the same procedures as their full-time colleagues. Part-time tutors working in LEA or WEA contexts increasingly find themselves absorbed by the audit culture that is so familiar to those of us who work in larger institutions. But what about the self-employed tutor? How do they experience the demands of evaluation? Put simply, they don't, unless as part of a personal commitment to constantly reviewing and exploring the nature of their professional practice. That is to say, by being a reflective practitioner, such tutors engage with internally driven, rather than externally imposed, discussions about the quality of what they do.

A short note on quality assurance

Policies and procedures for evaluation of assessment (and indeed evaluation of teaching and learning in colleges in its broadest sense) are normally organised within a single, strategic approach. The management and coordination of these different evaluation activities is not left to chance. Different stakeholders communicate on a regular basis and all work towards an overall scheme for ensuring the quality of educational provision. This approach is called 'quality assurance'.

'Quality assurance', 'total quality management', 'quality assessment' – terms like these, originally found in a business context, have been a common feature within the education community for many years now. Although there is no fixed definition of quality in education, the use of the word tends to imply an active concern, on the part of tutors, colleges and awarding bodies, to provide the best service possible for the customers – the learners. Programmes of study must be rigorous, well-resourced and offer value for money. Teachers and trainers must have up-to-date qualifications and experience. The programme must be fit for the purpose for which it was intended, meeting agreed levels of performance or agreed outcomes (also known as standards).

Quality assurance is an area of research and study in its own right, beyond the scope of this book. Suggestions for further reading in this area are at the end of this chapter.

A SUMMARY OF **KEY POINTS**

In this chapter, we have looked at the following key themes:
> **the importance of evaluation in education and specifically in assessment procedure and practice;**
> **methodologies for carrying out evaluation in a range of formal and informal contexts;**
> **the stakeholders involved in evaluation;**
> **the role of evaluation in helping to develop and improve assessment practice.**

Evaluation operates on two distinct, overlapping, levels. It is embedded within the formal policies and procedures of colleges, awarding bodies, funding agencies and government departments, and enshrined in practices like Total Quality Management (TQM) and organisations like Investors In People (IiP). For the new teacher or trainer, encountering all these initiatives for the first time can be bewildering. But if we remember that we need to be responsible for evaluation in a more personal capacity, in the informal contexts described above, then the benefits of careful evaluation will become self-evident.

Branching options

Reflection
What are your experiences and understandings of the evaluation frameworks that underpin your curriculum or organisation? Are you aware of how evaluation works, and why, or is it an activity that is more or less hidden from view?

Analysis
Evaluation and accountability go hand in hand to some extent, although it is important to remember that the process of evaluation in itself need not be seen as intrusive. At one level,

reflective practice can be seen as a form of highly personalised and personal evaluation. As such, evaluation can be seen as being a key concept of assessment practice irrespective of the organisational context within which it takes place. If you are a full-time tutor in a large college, do you find time and space for more personal evaluation? If you are a part-time tutor working in adult education, does such evaluation form a conscious part of your work?

Research

Key concepts such as validity and reliability apply to evaluation as much as they apply to the assessment process. Using both your library resources and the internet, explore the extent to which evaluation is a focus of research activity. Is evaluation critically examined, or is it taken for granted?

REFERENCES AND FURTHER READING REFERENCES AND FURTHER READING

Ashcroft, K and Palacio, D (1996) *Researching into Assessment and Evaluation in Colleges and Universities*. London: Kogan Page.

Commons, P K (2003) 'The Contribution of Inspection, Self-assessment, Investors in People and the Inclusive Learning Quality Initiative to Improving Quality in Further Education Sector Colleges: an initial exploration', *Journal of Further and Higher Education* 27 (1) pp27-46.

Sallis, E and Hingley, P (1992) *Total Quality Management*. Bristol: Staff College.

Scott, G (2010) Institutional issues: the college of further education as a twenty-first century organisation, in Wallace, S (ed.) *The Lifelong Learning Sector Reflective Reader*. Exeter: Learning Matters.

9

Equality of opportunity and inclusive practice

By the end of this chapter you should:

- be able to evaluate ways in which tutors should take into consideration the particular needs or requirements of learners with learning difficulties or disabilities when planning for assessment;
- be aware of the opportunities for additional support that are available when facilitating assessment for learners.

Professional Standards

This chapter relates to the following Professional Standards.

Professional Values

ES2: Assessing the work of learners in a fair and equitable manner.

Professional Knowledge and Understanding

EK2.1: Issues of equality and diversity in assessment.

Professional Practice

EP2.1: Apply appropriate methods of assessment fairly and effectively.

Making education available to all

Meeting a learner who uses a wheelchair, a learner who is accompanied by a sign language interpreter, or a learner who has another member of staff helping them on a one-to-one basis is an increasingly common sight in the Lifelong Learning sector. Happily, social attitudes towards people with disabilities are changing, propelled by government initiatives and legislation, and it is no longer acceptable practice for learners with disabilities to be excluded from mainstream educational opportunities and restricted to education in special schools and colleges. Learners with disabilities can be accommodated, thanks to technology and to the changing attitudes of society.

Some of the ways in which technology can help disabled learners have only recently become widely available. The growing use and greater affordability of computers is one example. A partially-sighted learner can use a computer with a greatly magnified screen display. A learner with restricted mobility can use a computer with speech recognition software to create written documents. Other technologies are less revolutionary, however: a blind or partially-sighted learner can have coursework materials provided on audio cassette or compact disc, while a learner who uses a wheelchair may need ramps and lifts in order to access a classroom.

> **PRACTICAL TASK** PRACTICAL TASK PRACTICAL TASK PRACTICAL TASK PRACTICAL TASK
>
> There are a number of case studies throughout this chapter, some with activities attached. As you work through the cases you will come across a number of practical solutions for helping learners with a range of disabilities and difficulties, some of which would be the responsibility of the provider, and others the responsibility of the teacher or trainer. Keep a note as you read the whole chapter of all the steps that can be taken by teachers to support learners with disabilities.

The role of Learning Support

Teachers and trainers need to be aware of the issues and difficulties faced by learners with disabilities and there are lots of things that we can do to accommodate them in our classes. Sometimes we may simply need to redesign handouts (to help learners with dyslexia, for example) or rearrange furniture (to allow access for learners with impaired mobility). At other times, we will need to consult and receive help from other members of staff who have specialist skills, qualifications and experience in providing the help and facilities needed by learners with disabilities. This provision is referred to as Learning Support.

The exact support provided for learners will vary from person to person. It may be necessary for tutors to change aspects of their course, such as teaching methods or resources. The learner may also need specialist resources and this is where the Learning Support department will be able to help. Learning support workers are also involved in:

- **the identification and diagnosis of specific learning difficulties or disabilities (see Chapter 2);**
- **the provision of additional tutorial support, normally on a one-to-one basis;**
- **the provision of additional care support. This normally involves someone providing mobility or physical support, help with specialist equipment and personal care, and emotional support. Frequently, care support workers such as this would attend sessions with the learner, rather than just providing support outside of class time.**

> **PRACTICAL TASK** PRACTICAL TASK PRACTICAL TASK PRACTICAL TASK PRACTICAL TASK
>
> It is important for all tutors to know about the facilities available to them in order to help learners with disabilities access education and training. If you are currently working in a large organisation, talk to a colleague or mentor about what is available. If you are a part-time adult or community education tutor, how might the organisation for whom you work be able to provide appropriate support for a learner with a disability?

The Equality Act

Additional impetus to allow learners with disabilities to access mainstream education comes from government legislation. In 2001, the Special Educational Needs and Disability Act (SENDA) was introduced, and from September 2003, a new section of the Disability Discrimination Act (DDA) came into force. According to this legislation (referred to as the DDA Part Four), all providers of post-compulsory education were legally obliged not to discriminate against learners with disabilities. In 2010, a new Equality Act was introduced by the then Labour government, which superseded not only the DDA, but other older legislation relating to, for example, racial discrimination, as well. The terms of the Equality Act impact on all aspects of the educational provision offered by further education providers, and outlaws discriminatory or unfavourable treatment from the point of enrolment, to the point of qualification and beyond. The Act requires all further education providers (which include not only colleges but also private training providers, or indeed any organisation that offers any formal provision that is endorsed by an appropriate body) to make *reasonable adjustments* so that discriminatory treatment is avoided. Such adjustments may relate to the ways in which actual courses or modules are delivered, but they may also relate to wider services provided by the college, such as financial help or counselling services. That is to say, *all* of the different aspects of the further education curriculum (courses, support services, accommodation and so on) are subject to the Act. In addition, colleges need to ensure that they provide equality of access and service for all students, irrespective of whether or not they have a disability (that may or may not have been disclosed by the individual), and for any other people who may have access to college facilities, but who are not actually enrolled as students within that institution.

Reading government legislation and working out the exact differences between learners with learning difficulties and learners with disabilities can be a time-consuming exercise and difficult for the non-specialist. We will concentrate here on practical responses that can help any learners with a disability or a learning difficulty participate in assessment.

Equality of opportunity: assessment practice

Admitting learners with disabilities has affected many aspects of the role of the teacher or trainer in the post-compulsory sector. There would be little point in admitting a learner who is unable to write to a sociology course, only for them to fall at the final hurdle because the course assessment is based on a written project. The law obliges awarding and examining bodies to adapt their methods and practices. If you are planning a formative assessment activity, then it will be down to you – as the tutor – to ensure that any learners with disabilities can participate, in just the same way that you may need to alter or change other teaching and learning methods. Only the awarding body can authorise changes to summative or formative assessments for a learner with disabilities or learning difficulties. They have a range of policies in place for this, but they have to be followed to the letter. Even if you are the first to realise that assessments may need to be altered, you will not be expected to make all the arrangements yourself. FE colleges have an office or department responsible for coordinating all the examinations that learners take within the college. The examinations office will work with the awarding body, the learner and the tutor to set up any additional resources or change any procedures as required. Community-based tutors will need to liaise with their employers, and for part-time tutors who are not in everyday contact with their employer, such a process can be time-consuming.

REFLECTIVE TASK

Read through the following two case studies. As you do so, consider the jobs you might need to do and the people you may need to talk to within a college, adult education centre or other training environment in order to help make all the arrangements that might be needed to help the learners in question. You may like to ask your mentor for guidance.

CASE STUDY 1

A learner on an Access course at a local college has difficulty with some aspects of her work. She has a form of dyslexia that makes reading difficult. In the past, she has found that printed materials produced with a large typeface on pale yellow or pale green paper make reading easier. Despite several requests to her tutor, however, nothing has happened, and she is still receiving the same handouts as the other learners – white paper with small fonts. The first written assessment, a 1500 word essay, is due to be submitted in two weeks' time and she is feeling apprehensive about having to produce a relatively lengthy piece of written work.

CASE STUDY 2

A learner who is deaf began studying towards an accountancy qualification five weeks ago. A British Sign Language (BSL) interpreter, provided through the college learning support office, supports him during taught sessions and at certain other times of the week for private study. The tutor runs lively sessions, involving lots of question-and-answer activities. However, the tutor does not include the deaf learner in these activities. When the group is engaged in individual work, like calculations, the tutor moves around the group, asking questions on a one-to-one basis and checking progress. Once again, the deaf learner is excluded and his work has never been checked in this manner.

In the first case study, the Access tutor could easily have avoided discriminatory behaviour simply by producing his printed materials in a different format. This could be done very easily using a word processor and coloured paper, or by asking for clerical help if the tutor does not have the necessary word-processing skills. The tutor could consult the learning support office for guidance. The Access tutor is simply being asked to arrange for some handouts to be produced in a slightly different format. This is not a complicated procedure and although it may take some time to organise a delay of several weeks is not acceptable. The learner is facing genuine problems in completing the first formal assignment. This could be a formative or summative assessment: either way, she is being excluded. In fact, there are two problems for us to consider here: first, the learner's access to the materials that she needs so that she can attempt the work; second, the assessment task itself. Her ability is not the issue here but the tutor needs to consider whether or not she may need a little more time to complete the assignment as it stands, or whether an alternative assessment format – such as a series of short-answer questions – would be more suitable.

In the second case study, the accountancy tutor is undermining the good work already done by the institution. The provision of a BSL interpreter is all well and good, but unless the tutor changes her approach, the deaf learner will continue to experience discriminatory behaviour: the learner is being treated less favourably by the tutor as a result of his disability. The accountancy tutor's behaviour may be due to a number of factors. It may be the case that she is genuinely unsure of how to work with a deaf learner, perhaps through inexperience. She may have assumed that, with a BSL interpreter in place, she would not have to worry about the learner. However, the presence of a learning support worker is not, on its own, enough to guarantee inclusive practice. In this situation, the learner is excluded from informal assessment and feedback by the tutor's behaviour. He will miss out on formative assessment activity (questions and answers) and developmental feedback during the calculation exercises. The issue here is tutor behaviour: with some changes to current practice, the deaf learner could be included in discussion and feedback.

Both of these case studies highlight the fact that as teachers and trainers, we have a part to play in not only diagnosing but also planning for and adjusting to learners with disabilities. We may need to change our resources, our handouts, our methods and our assessments. Above all, we may need to change our attitude.

Supporting our learners

Tailoring assessment methods will not just involve learners with disabilities. Learners who have undergone a diagnostic assessment (as discussed in Chapter 2) and been identified as having specific learning needs and requirements will also need to have adjustments made in assessment. A learner may be aware of the support that they need, possibly (but not necessarily) as a result of previous diagnosis or educational experience. Here, the learning support office is vital. It is important to remember, however, that the onus will sometimes be on us, as teachers and trainers, to take the first steps in meeting the learner's needs. Learners with disabilities or with particular needs are not obliged to seek extra support prior to enrolment, and are entitled to confidentiality.

Alterations and adjustments may involve redesigning our formative assessment activities to enable full participation or perhaps creating a new range of assessment activities that meet a variety of needs. They may involve submissions to the awarding or accrediting body if formal summative assessment arrangements need to be modified. We may need to look around for resources and support within our own institution. Our responses will depend on the exact needs of the learner: there are no one-size-fits-all strategies.

Teachers and trainers have varying degrees of flexibility, depending on the context in which they work. First of all, we need to inform potential learners of the opportunities available for adapting and/or redesigning assessment activities before enrolment: lack of awareness of flexible provision is often cited as a significant barrier to participation for learners with disabilities. If we are designing formative assessments for use during our own sessions, our choice of method is up to us. If we are designing a summative assessment, however, we must ensure that our chosen method meets the learning outcomes that the awarding body has put in place.

Making adjustments for formative assessment

CASE STUDY 1
Tony is an ICT lecturer working with adult learners on a range of programmes at levels 1 and 2. He is writing a lesson plan for the next session of a beginners' computer class. The aim of the session is to introduce the learners to email and he has designed the following formative assessment activity.

Email exercise
1. Please send an email to me at this address: tonytutor@college.ac.uk. In the email, I would like you to write a few sentences about what you have learned on the course so far. Which topic was the most enjoyable? Have you found any topics difficult?

2. After I have received your email, I will send you a reply.

3. After you receive my reply, I would like you to print your message and my reply. Collect your printout from the printer, place it in your progress file and then hand your file in to me.

In his learning journal, Tony reflected on the activity.

The email exercise went really well. All nine learners sent their emails to me, and it was really useful to read what they wrote about the course so far – it was a good way to get feedback. I had no idea that the grammar checker was causing such uproar! All the group have got hold of the basics, although a couple of them are a bit stuck on some of the word processing functions. That doesn't matter too much, because they are all using individual learning plans so I can easily tailor the activities to suit them. Everything went fine – no printer jams or crashes today, thankfully, although Patrick almost knocked over the network printer when reaching for his work. I was really careful not to make a thing out of it though – it's just because of his disability. He seemed fine about it and I quickly put everything back.

The assessment activity in itself is fine: by keeping the content of the email focused on a subject that all the group can comment on equally – the course so far – Tony has shown a good degree of awareness of inclusive practice. It is easy, when designing simple assessments such as this, to pick on what might be seen as everyday topics that in fact inadvertently discriminate against some members of the group. For example, asking for an email about 'The last holiday I took with my husband/wife' would run the risk of discriminating against a member of the group who was unmarried, whatever their background. Tony's attention to detail has not extended to the layout of his classroom, however. Patrick is a wheelchair user and is clearly finding himself having to stretch a little too far for comfort when reaching for his work. Ideally, Tony's response would be to move the printer so that all the members of the group could have access to it. This may be something that Tony can do himself, or it may be something that he needs to refer to another department of the institution, such as the IT technical support department.

Case Study 2

Claire is a lecturer in travel and tourism, teaching courses at levels 2 and 3. Her learners are assessed in a variety of ways, including written work, portfolio-based assessment and observation in workplace settings. She has drawn up a written exercise for her group, one of whom has dyslexia. On her lesson plans, she always has a 'notes' section, which for this session reads as follows.

NB Jackie's test paper – pale green A4 and Arial 14, allow an extra day.

This note illustrates a common strategy for learners with dyslexia (although, of course, there are different forms of dyslexia and this is not an adjustment that would work for everyone). Claire produces all printed materials on coloured paper and in a large font for Jackie, in order to enhance the readability of the document. And in recognition of the extra time it takes Jackie to complete written work, because it takes her longer both to read and research her answers and then to write them, Claire has decided on a short extension to the deadline.

Jackie's case raises a further question. Do you think that Claire should produce all of her handouts and quiz sheets using pale green paper and Arial 14 for the whole group?

If Claire produced the same handout for everyone, Jackie would not be seen as receiving different treatment from everyone else. Perhaps the fact that Jackie always receives pale green papers draws attention to her dyslexia? Then again, if there were a second learner with dyslexia in the group, it would not automatically be the case that pale green paper would be the most appropriate strategy for him or her. They may prefer to use a tinted acetate sheet placed over a handout, or wear glasses with tinted lenses. One of the ideas that underpin differentiation in post-compulsory education is the fact that, as teachers and trainers, we should not treat all our learners in the same way. Inclusive practice is not about treating everyone the same: it is about taking the necessary steps to allow all learners access to education and training opportunities, irrespective of whether or not the barrier to participation is disability, social background or personal circumstances.

Formative assessment: checklist for inclusivity

When planning for formal formative assessment, use the following checklist to help evaluate your assessment methods.

- If you have learners with physical or mental health difficulties, or learning difficulties, have you asked them about strategies that they have found effective in the past? This may help you to plan appropriate assessment activities.
- Have you taken account of any extra equipment or time a disabled learner may need? Sometimes, a simple adjustment such as organising the provision of a magnifying reading lamp (for example) will be all that is needed. On other occasions, sophisticated computer equipment may be needed but remember that using speech recognition software when word-processing an assignment may take extra time.
- Have you taken into consideration the location in which the assessment will be run? If you are asking your learners to take part in a study project in your college's learning resource centre, are all the books and materials within reach? The learning resource centre could be an intimidating environment for a learner with mental health difficulties, who may feel anxiety if asked to work in an unfamiliar location.
- Has the assignment brief been made available in an appropriate format? As well as a printed version of the assessment, you may need to provide details in an alternative format, such as on a CD or USB memory stick.
- Have you considered how you might make contact with other professionals who might be able to help? In a college, the learning support office will be happy to help organise resources, provide learning support assistants and generally offer advice.
- Does the assessment still meet your learning outcomes? The important thing to remember (and this is the case with summative assessment as well) is that as teachers and trainers, we are helping all of our learners to reach the intended learning outcomes for the class or session. If our learners will still meet the outcomes by using an alternative or modified assessment activity, then we can go ahead and use it.

And when thinking about the informal formative assessment methods that you use, consider these issues.

- During questions and answers or discussion, do you make allowances for learners who risk being excluded? This could involve changing the way you speak, for example, by speaking slowly and avoiding technical language, or positioning yourself away from harsh light if someone is trying to lip-read.
- Remember to address questions or comments directly to the learner and not to the learning support assistant.
- If you have a learner with a speech difficulty in your group, allow them time to finish answering – do not finish sentences for them. If they are reticent about participating, avoid questions that require long answers and provide some thinking time.
- Write questions and their answers on the board, remembering not to talk while facing away from the group. If a learner has difficulty in keeping up-to-speed when writing down answers, you will need to consider ways in which they can be helped. If the attendance of a learning support assistant is not appropriate, you could consider using audio recordings, or asking for one of the group to be the official note-taker, and supplying photocopies of notes at the start of the following class.
- If you have a learner with an autistic spectrum disorder (such as Asperger's syndrome) in your group, they may respond better to written than oral questions.

REFLECTIVE TASK

Go back to the Reflective task on page 49. Reread the assessment methods that you listed and consider the ways in which they might need to be adjusted for learners with different disabilities. Consider alternative assessment methods if necessary.

Making adjustments for summative assessment

Formative assessment is very much down to the individual teacher or trainer: we have a great deal of control about when and how we assess our learners in this manner. Summative assessment, on the other hand, is very often restricted by the awarding or accrediting body. This restriction may be in the method of assessment employed (as many awarding bodies dictate exactly how a module or course is assessed), the timing of the assessment (normally at the end of the module or programme of study) and the location (which for an exam would normally be a controlled environment with an invigilator). Ensuring that a learner with a physical or mental health disability or a learning difficulty has access to assessment can involve time-consuming procedures and a lot of planning and preparation.

Let us return to Claire, the travel and tourism lecturer. In this extract from her learning diary, she reflects on the changes to the standard assessment that she has made to prevent Jackie, who is dyslexic, from being excluded.

Now that the group have all been signed off, it's funny to think back to all the panic over Jackie. I was really worried that she wouldn't get through the course, but the LSA (learning support assistant) was great – it was his idea that I get in touch with the external verifier and she helped me to organise all the form-filling and told me where to send the official psychologist's report. That report was all thanks to the LSA as well – he made all the arrangements. I just didn't realise that it would be so straightforward. And this was the first time that Jackie had been properly diagnosed – she was never tested like this during her time at school. That may be why she didn't enjoy it very much and left as soon as she could.

The three of us had a series of tutorials and I explained how the course was going to be assessed. The LSA made notes about which parts of the assessment could be done differently and that all went into my letter to the awarding body. And it was his idea to substitute the short-answer test for the interview. That had to be written up in advance and submitted to the examining board too. The college provided all the computer equipment as well. They even sent someone over to work the video camera when I did Jackie's interview.

Jackie was nervous about being filmed. I know how she felt! I was filmed when I did a micro-teach session for my Cert Ed. We did a dry run so that she could settle her nerves and avoid any silly mistakes.

CLOSE FOCUS **CLOSE** FOCUS **CLOSE** FOCUS **CLOSE** FOCUS **CLOSE** FOCUS

Having read this extract, make a note of the separate issues raised by Jackie's dyslexia and the strategies that were put in place to deal with it.

Claire's experiences highlight several examples of good practice:

- **the role played by learning support within her organisation – teachers and trainers are not expected to work in isolation;**
- **the need to inform the awarding body about any particular learner's needs or requirements in plenty of time (in this case, Claire's first point of call was the external verifier);**
- **the requirement to bring in external expertise (an educational psychologist assessed Jackie, and the ensuing report was required by the awarding body as evidence to support the claim for adapting the assessment procedure);**
- **the substitution of one assessment tool (a short-answer written paper) for another (an interview) – both met the required learning outcomes in this case, so the change was approved by the awarding body;**
- **the need for specialist equipment when conducting the assessment;**
- **the need to rehearse with specialist equipment so that the learner is supported and not disadvantaged by it.**

The significant difference between planning for formative assessment and planning for summative assessment is the role of external bodies: all the other issues (learning support, differentiation in assessment activity, use of specialist equipment) are found in both. Although a learner may choose to be assessed by an educational psychologist (assuming this is relevant to the learner's needs), it is by no means compulsory prior to enrolling on a course. In Jackie's case, however, the awarding body has insisted that the request for modification to the summative assessment process is accompanied by a psychologist's report. It is quite common for such requests to be accompanied by medical, or other, statements.

Different awarding bodies operate a variety of procedures relating to candidates with particular requirements. These guidelines may be included within the documentation or handbooks for a specific course or programme of study, or they may be found in separate policy documents. Broadly speaking, learners' requirements are categorised under some or all of the following headings:

- **learners who are physically disabled;**
- **learners who are blind or partially sighted;**

- learners who are deaf or partially hearing;
- learners with specific learning difficulties (for example, dyslexia or dyspraxia);
- learners with mental health difficulties (for example, clinical and/or environmental depression);
- learners with other medical conditions that require consideration (for example, epilepsy).

However, not all the learners with specific needs whom we may meet will fit neatly into one of these categories. Learners may have specific learning difficulties as a consequence of another physical disability or other medical condition. For example, a learner may take medication to help with a mental health condition and the side effect of that medication may be loss of concentration over extended periods of time. Another learner may have received an injury that has to be treated permanently with medication that causes considerable discomfort. Our responsibility as teachers and trainers is to treat all of our learners as individuals. But very often treatment of disabled learners continues to be stereotypical when we should really be tailoring our responses to individuals' needs.

Summative assessment: checklist for inclusivity

There are many potential actions and resources available to our learners when adapting summative assessments, therefore, some of which will overlap.

Provision of extra time
This may be necessary to accommodate learners who are using specialist IT equipment, who have difficulty writing quickly because of a physical disability or who are dyslexic and need more time to complete written assignments.

Provision of specialist equipment
A learner who is partially sighted may require special computer software that will allow the screen display to be magnified, a Dictaphone or a talking calculator. A learner who is deaf may use a hearing aid but not all classrooms and workshops are fitted with induction loops and stand-alone equipment will be necessary. It is important to remember that the learner may require practice in using specialist equipment, so that the equipment itself does not become a hindrance during the assessment. If possible, arrange for any new equipment to be tested well in advance of an assessment activity.

Provision of specialised learning support
Learners may require the help of a communicator or interpreter (for example, for British Sign Language), a writer/note-taker and/or a reader. These learning support assistants may require specific advice or even training if the assessment involves technical language or procedures that may be new to them.

Provision of adjusted or redesigned assessment activities
This may involve negotiating a wholly different assessment activity, such as substituting an oral-based assignment for a written assignment. It may also involve the provision of assessment tasks using alternative media, for example the production of an assignment paper in large text, Braille or raised type, or on audio cassette. A reader and/or writer may be provided so that the learner can dictate her/his answers.

Provision of an alternative location
If the room that has been allocated for an examination is not accessible, then an alternative room will need to be found. Some learners with mental health difficulties may find the stress

of sitting an examination in a large room unbearable. This could be alleviated simply by allowing the learner to visit the room in advance and become acclimatised to it, or it may be necessary to find an alternative venue. If another learner is using equipment or receiving help from a learning support assistant, the noise or movement generated may cause distractions that will be detrimental to the other learners present.

CASE STUDY

Read through the following case study and then consider answers to the questions that follow.

Julie is a tutor on an access to higher education diploma, accredited by AQA. She specialises in teaching study skills. When designing the assessment requirements for the unit, she and the other members of the access team decided that there would be three elements for learners to complete:

- a portfolio, made up of written work completed during the course, as well as other evidence of achievement;
- a short written task completed during the course;
- an extended written task completed by the end of the course.

1. Is the assessment currently accessible to a range of learners with different disabilities/needs or would Julie have to change or adapt her methods?
2. What actions could Julie take to change or adapt the assessment on her own? For what actions do you think that she might need to ask for guidance and advice from other professionals?
3. What could Julie do to make the measures that have been designed to increase access to the course known to potential learners with disabilities?

Looking at these assignments in the light of inclusive practice raises a number of issues. They are all heavily biased towards written work. If one of Julie's learners experiences difficulty in completing written work an alternative method may be needed. One of the learners may be experiencing difficulty in completing written work because they take medication that affects their concentration. Can an extension to the deadline be arranged? If the assignments need to be researched independently, are the research materials (either print or online) accessible? This could require simple arrangements, such as organising books to be shelved at a height that everyone can reach or remembering to organise access to computers (this often needs to be booked in advance).

In essence, it is all about thinking ahead. Much of our practice as teachers and trainers relies on careful preparation – of resources, learning materials and assessment. If we are aware of the needs of all of our learners, and knowing where and from whom we can find appropriate support, we can ensure inclusive practice at all times.

A SUMMARY OF **KEY POINTS**

In this chapter, we have looked at the following key themes:

> **the impact of the 2010 Equality Act on post-compulsory education and training;**
> **inclusive strategies for organising and modifying formative assessment;**
> **inclusive strategies for organising and modifying summative assessment;**

> **> the role played by other professionals in ensuring inclusivity in assessment.**
>
> Adjusting practice to meet learners' particular requirements necessitates a personal and an institutional commitment. Despite the fact that legislation, technology and attitudes are all changing, learners with disabilities are still under-represented in post-compulsory education and training. As teachers and trainers, we cannot do everything, nor are we expected to. But as practitioners in classrooms and workshops, we are often the first point of call for the learner, and we can work hard to change our attitudes and be proactive in making adjustments to our assessment practice that will facilitate wider participation.

Branching options

Reflection

Look through the resources that accompany the teacher training course that you are currently undertaking. Make a note of the different assessment activities that you will complete. Do they model inclusive practice? If not, why not?

Analysis

It is important for tutors to be proactive, and to anticipate learner needs. Learners are not obliged to inform tutors of any disability, and whilst some disabilities are conspicuous, unseen disabilities such as mental health difficulties or dyspraxia, may not be so obvious. How might the materials and activities that you employ in your assessment practice be adapted to anticipate any such needs?

Research

Disability issues are both a focus for research in their own right, as well as a key aspect of research into widening participation, and it is worth browsing academic journals for case studies. In addition to this, make contact with the person or people within your organisation who have responsibility for working with learners with specific needs and talk to them. Are there any recent examples of best practice within your organisation that you can learn from?

REFERENCES AND FURTHER READING

Kennedy, H (1997) *Learning Works: Widening Participation in Further Education*. Coventry: Further Education Funding Council.

National Institute for Adult Continuing Education (2003) *New Rights To Learn: a tutor guide to teaching adults after the Disability Discrimination Act Part 4*. Leicester: NIACE.

Sanderson, A (2001) 'Disabled Students in Transition: a tale of two sectors' failure to communicate', *Journal of Further and Higher Education* 25 (2), 2001 pp227-240.

Smith, C (2009) From special needs to inclusive education, in Sharp, J, Ward, S and Hankin, L (eds.) *Education Studies: an issues-based approach*. Second edition. Exeter: Learning Matters.

Wright, A-M, Abdi-Jama, S, Colquhon, S, Speare, J and Partridge, T (2006) *FE Lecturer's Guide to Diversity and Inclusion*. London: Continuum.

10
ILT and e-assessment

By the end of this chapter you should:

- **know about the role of Information and Learning Technology (ILT) in the assessment process;**
- **be able to evaluate the role of computer-based technologies in: managing assessment; as an assessment medium; as a tool to open assessment up to broader audiences.**

Professional Standards

This chapter relates to the following Professional Standards.

Professional Values

ES1: Designing and using assessment as a tool for learning and progression.

Professional Knowledge and Understanding

EK1.2: Ways to devise, select, use and appraise assessment tools, including, where appropriate, those which exploit new and emerging technologies.

Professional Practice

EP1.2: Devise, select, use and appraise assessment tools including, where appropriate, those which exploit new and emerging technologies.

A short note about abbreviations

We often encounter abbreviations and acronyms in computers and computing technology. There are three common abbreviations in computing: IT, ICT and ILT. IT is information technology. This term is used to refer to the equipment, hardware and software that we use – computers, scanners, disk drives and software programs are all covered by this term. ICT is information and communication technology. This term refers to the combination of computing technology with communications technology – telephones, computer networks and wireless links. ICT allows computers to communicate with each other at a local level (for example, the use of a computer network within a college that allows tutors and learners to log on at any computer terminal within the college and access work that has been previously saved) and at a global level (the world wide web). ILT is information and learning technology. ILT does not just refer to computer terminals and the software that runs on them, but to other technology as well. We shall return to a discussion of ILT resources later.

PRACTICAL TASK PRACTICAL TASK **PRACTICAL TASK** PRACTICAL TASK **PRACTICAL TASK**

Before reading on, spend a few moments writing down all the different uses of ILT that you have encountered as a teacher-training learner. As you read through this list, consider the extent to which you would make the same uses of ILT as a teacher. Would you feel confident in using ILT or would you need additional support or training? Do you think that some areas of the curriculum require a greater use of ILT than others?

Now turn back to Chapter 2 and reread the section on specific aptitude assessments: functional skills (page 18).

In Chapter 2, we read about the experiences of two trainee teachers – David and Ann – who had completed a computer-based assessment of their literacy and numeracy skills. In the following journal extract their lecturer, Julie, reflects on the diagnostic assessment of the teacher-training group as a whole.

My first concern was the actual organisation of the assessment. Because we are only a few weeks into the term, not all of the learners have organised their passwords for the network yet, so I had to organise temporary passwords so that they could all log on. Then I had to timetable the tests. In the end I had to run a week later than I had hoped because I couldn't get a booking. I had no idea that the computers got booked up so fast – but I guess it's fair enough because most of them are just for drop-in use and if they were all reserved then none of the learners would get to use them without difficulty. And then I had to work out where the printers were and copy an instruction sheet for the tests and it all seemed to take a disproportionate amount of time.

My other real worry was how the learners would react when they got their feedback. You don't have to be a functional skills tutor to know that learners are often apprehensive about assessments in maths and English. There were a couple of surprises actually. One of the group – David – told me afterwards that he'd been really nervous about his literacy score. It was a classic case of being told at school that he was no good and that just stuck with him afterwards. He said that his result was better than he had expected. Ann was a different story and had been really nervous about both of the tests, especially numeracy. During her tutorial, she told me that she had hated doing maths at school, so at that stage I was thinking along the same lines as I had done when talking to lots of other learners – prior experience as a barrier to learning. But then she said something else that really made me stop in my tracks, which was that she was even more nervous because she was having to sit the test using a computer. She doesn't have a PC at home, and has never had to use one for her work.

It's blindingly obvious in hindsight, but I just didn't think of it at the time. I was so wrapped up in the technology – instant feedback and no marking – that I didn't consider the simple fact that if you were a fluent computer user, you would find the test easier to do compared to someone who didn't really use a PC at all. Ann said to me afterwards that she was sure that if she sat the test again, now that she had had a lot of practice on the computer and had let the experience sink in, she would get a better score. So much for my validity and reliability!

Julie's reflections about the computer-based assessment can be broadly divided into two categories. First, there is the issue of the management and application of the assessment – the bookings, the instant results and the absence of yet more marking. Second, there is the process of assessment itself and the extent to which using a computer-based assessment, rather than a paper-based assessment, helps or hinders the diagnostic process. There are undoubtedly benefits: the entire process of assessment, marking and feedback has been significantly accelerated and the burden of paperwork on the tutor has been reduced. The marks and feedback can be stored electronically for retrieval at a later stage. A computer-based assessment might also have been preferable for some of the learners. Memories of paper-based examinations can be difficult for some learners to deal with and the computer-based format may help overcome this. But unless all the learners are suffi-ciently, if not equally, proficient in using computers, then the validity and reliability of the process cannot be guaranteed.

E-assessment

The increasing use of ILT is inevitable: it is a reflection of the ever greater use of technology in all walks of life. However, it is important to remember that the ability to use IT (possession of IT skills is often referred to as IT literacy) is not just restricted to the world of work. More and more people use the internet and email at home, to book holidays, to buy and listen to music, or buy and sell used goods. As technology advances, work and social lives adapt, and education and training plays a part in both.

Of course, there is more to ILT than simply providing facilities and activities for courses and programmes of study that have IT at the centre of their curriculum. Whether we are referring to a course for trainee graphic designers who hope to work in industry, or to a course that is aimed at providing new computer owners with a friendly introduction to email, the role of ILT within the course is identical, even if the purpose of the two courses is very different. The graphic design course needs to replicate the real world of work. Content and assessment need to draw on current industry practices and standards in order to ensure authenticity and relevance. However, the authenticity and relevance of the introduction to email course is no less crucial. The difference is in the end product: the design course is aimed at future practitioners in a specific industrial or business context. The email course is aimed at people who wish to use email for more personal reasons.

It is to those areas of the curriculum that are not directly linked to technology that we need to turn. If, as tutors in the Lifelong Learning sector, we are to embrace and use ILT as an integral aspect of our working lives, then we need to consider why it is important to do so. We have touched on some of these issues at earlier stages in this book: a reflection, perhaps, of the way in which ILT has become integrated into everyday working practice.

Six reasons for using ILT

1. Assessment can be supplied as and when learners are ready

One of the most startling consequences of the widespread use of ILT is in assessment on demand. This is already a commonly-found feature in computer courses delivered in an open-learning format where learners can decide to take their summative assessment when they feel ready to do so. As well as encouraging self-assessment, transferring the decision about when an assessment should be completed from the tutor to the learner is empower-ing for the learner, encouraging greater ownership of the assessment process and the learning process as a whole. Many adult learners, in particular, are wary of the imposition of assessment regimes and deadlines. Moving the assessment deadline to 'when you feel that you are ready' has obvious and attractive benefits.

2. Results and feedback can be provided immediately

One of the factors that attracted Julie to the online literacy and numeracy diagnostic assessment that we discussed above was the speed with which feedback and results could be given to learners: in this case, it was immediate. As soon as they had finished the test, the learners could view their results and feedback on screen, and then send those results to the printer so that a hard copy could be generated (this might well find its way into their portfolios). Some computer courses offer similarly quick marking and feedback. Once again, the benefits are obvious: the nerve-wracking wait for results is replaced by an immediate response. This can be good news for tutors, and for colleges in general: for example, action planning or the provision of learning support following diagnostic assessment can begin at once.

3. The reliability of marking can be ensured

Markers, assessors and verifiers are only human. Despite the proliferation of marking schemes, learning outcomes, moderation and second marking, there are still disagreements about marking and grading. And every now and then a tutor, who is assessing learner work at the end of a very busy day, can make a mistake. Assuming that there are no problems with the hardware and software, computer-based marking is immediate and highly reliable.

The use of computers for marking raises a number of questions, however. Marking multiple-choice tests or true/false questions may well be straightforward, but assessment strategies of this nature may not be suitable for all curricula areas at all levels, for example, assessing a longer piece of written work, such as an essay. Text comprehension software that can recognise key words and expressions may be the answer but at the time of writing these are not applicable in a general educational context.

4. The paperwork burden can be reduced for learners and tutors

Anything that promises to reduce the forms that a tutor has to complete and file away is bound to be popular. In theory, the electronic storage of results, feedback and other data relating to learner progress and achievement promises to simplify record-keeping, aid evaluation (by having all the relevant information at your fingertips) and reduce the physical space needed for storage. In practice, a paperless staff room is still some way away and communication between tutors and managers, providers and awarding bodies is still paper-based. However, innovations such as online entry of grades and marks, and associated online storage of learner records of achievement, are becoming more common within some educational organisations.

Similarly, the potential for the learner is recognised if not yet realised. The implementation of portfolio-based assessment is widely recognised as being needlessly burdensome for some learners. The use of the e-portfolio, as well as solving the problem of where to keep all the work generated by learners (bulging filing cabinets and overflowing shelves are a common sight, and shopping trolleys are often the most practicable vehicle for moving portfolios from room to room), can facilitate the creation of documentation that supports lifelong learning, as well as encouraging the development of relevant and authentic IT skills (see below).

5. ILT can widen participation in education and training

It is important to recognise that a lack of IT skills can be a barrier to participation for many learners, whether this is due to a lack of confidence, a lack of enthusiasm or a lack of opportunity. However, technology can be a powerful tool in helping people who would otherwise not be able to do so to engage in education and training.

There is a range of uses of ILT in widening participation, some of which have been explicitly addressed in earlier chapters of this book. Learners with disabilities, for example, can use technology to participate in programmes of study that would otherwise be difficult to engage with. ILT may be used by tutors, by learners, or by both in order to widen access. Learners who have difficulty writing can use speech recognition software to produce written work. Tutors can use or create resources in a range of formats – on paper and on screen – that can be quickly customised for a learner who is partially-sighted or has dyslexia.

There is more to ILT than simply facilitating the work done within colleges: ILT can also be used to take learning out of colleges and into communities. Laptop computers and wireless links to the internet can be used to turn a community centre or the function room of a pub into an IT suite. As equipment becomes increasingly portable, adult education centres and outreach centres can enjoy the ILT facilities that campuses and main college buildings take for granted. ILT has changed the provision of distance learning, and computers are used to create virtual classrooms where distance learners, who would often work in relative isolation, can now communicate with each other in a chat room or via email.

6. IT literacy is a valuable life and work skill

The fact that IT skills are located within the functional skills framework that is currently central to much 14-19 curricular provision tells us about the importance attached to IT literacy by colleges, awarding bodies, employers and the government. Just as we talk about functional levels of numeracy and literacy (that is to say, the basic numeracy and literacy skills needed for everyday life), so talk of functional IT skills is becoming increasingly common. The impetus for acquiring IT skills can come from many directions. It may be necessary to use a computer for a particular job. It may be desirable to use the internet to research a hobby. It may be necessary to acquire IT skills in order to help a child with homework. IT has spread into so many parts of our life, it seems perverse not to allow the same to happen within further education. Tutors can encourage learners to use the internet to carry out research projects (although guidance will be necessary, as we shall discuss below), or to use a word processor to complete a written assignment.

Learners use ILT at many stages of their learning careers, but when it comes to the assessment of learning, the technology is less well represented. A move towards greater use of ILT in summative assessment is, quite clearly, something that must await the leadership of awarding bodies and curriculum authorities. However, formative assessment (as discussed in Chapter 3) is often more directly under the control of the tutor. So what are the ILT strategies that can be employed to encourage e-assessment for learning?

The use of ILT in assessment

Blended assessment

'Blended' learning refers to the blending of ILT with 'traditional' teaching and learning. The term recognises that, in the first instance, ILT needs to be integrated into existing practice. Tutors and learners need to adapt to ILT on a gradual basis. There are many ways in which ILT use can be incorporated within existing strategies for formative assessment. Moreover, attractive materials can be produced with only a modest amount of technical know-how. If tutors are careful when organising small groups, peer-learning of new ILT skills can be encouraged.

Learner presentations can be delivered using PowerPoint

As well as providing learners with an opportunity to acquire or enhance IT skills within another curriculum area, the use of PowerPoint, or any other similar software, allows the presentations created to be stored, circulated and duplicated very easily.

Written work can be word processed

The use of word processors need not be restricted to essay-type questions. The production of posters and leaflets, for example, can often be suitable activities for formative assessment.

Small-scale research projects

These can be based on research carried out using the word wide web and can include a critical review of the websites that were used. Many tutors are reluctant to encourage web-based research at the expense of books and journals. The reason most frequently cited for this reluctance is quality control: it can be difficult to negotiate such a large resource as the word wide web and the quality of material to be found is variable, to say the least.

Email groups or chat room groups can be set up easily

These facilitate group discussions outside class contact time. Setting up an email group is a simple task and can allow tutor and learners to contact each other at different times. As an additional support strategy, this can be highly effective: some learners are more comfortable using the written word, rather than the spoken word, when articulating difficulties that they are experiencing with their work. Some tutors will accept draft submissions of assignments via email, and feedback can be delivered in the same way.

Strategies like these demand a certain amount of preparation on the part of the tutor. Tutors need to have sufficient basic ILT skills to help learners if they have difficulty in creating their presentations or their posters. It is important to be realistic, however: unless a tutor is an IT specialist, learners will not expect comprehensive technical support. But a basic understanding of the hardware and software used is essential. At the very least, tutors need to be able to use the same ILT materials that they are asking their learners to use and a basic level of technical knowledge (what plugs in where, what to do if a computer crashes, how to attach a data projector to a computer) will also be required.

Using the internet for research poses problems of a different order, however. As well as teaching learners the basic research skills needed for navigating such a huge resource, the issue of quality of content has to be dealt with. Here, advance preparation is necessary. You would not send your learners off to do research work in the learning resource centre without providing guidance on what resources to use, so if you are directing them towards internet research, you will have to supply lists of recommended websites. Many textbooks (including this one) provide suggestions for websites, and many educational or curriculum bodies and trade or industry organisations have extensive websites that can be used for research. By encouraging learners to evaluate the websites that they use, and to share their findings with their peers, tutors can encourage the development of transferable study skills.

In essence, blended-assessment strategies are the same as their non-ILT assisted equivalents. It isn't compulsory to use PowerPoint for peer presentations: an overhead projector or a flip chart pad will do. Learners may be encouraged to use a word processor, but a handwritten assignment is still perfectly acceptable. Despite this, a blended approach is to be encouraged, for the reasons mentioned earlier: the greater use of technology in education mirrors the greater use of technology in the home and the workplace. And, it could be argued, a greater use of technology is increasingly expected by our learners.

From blended assessment to e-assessment

If we are keen to explore valuable applications of e-assessment in our teaching and training practice, greater engagement with technology will be required. Some tutors are adept users of ILT and can learn quickly how to do new things; other tutors are less confident and may need training courses. Many education and training providers offer staff training in a range of areas, including ILT. For some tutors, enrolling on an accredited course such as ECDL (European Computer Driving Licence), perhaps as part of a broader Continuing Professional Development strategy, may be more appropriate. It may be necessary to ask specialist support staff for help. Specialist IT or ILT departments can provide technical support and advice on using the resources available, and may be willing to help create resources for tutors who are using ILT for the first time.

E-assessment, therefore, can be seen as distinct from blended assessment. I have used the term blended assessment to refer to situations and strategies for assessment where ILT use can be blended with existing practice. E-assessment refers to activities and strategies where ILT is an integral and essential component of the assessment activity, rather than a technological bolt-on. So what tools are available?

Technologies and strategies for supporting e-assessment

Virtual Learning Environments

A virtual learning environment (VLE) is a software package that is run on a network of computers. Blackboard and Moodle are good examples. Some VLEs are accessed through the internet. Other VLEs can only be accessed by tutors and learners at a specific college. In this situation, the VLE is found on the college computer network or intranet (a website that is only available inside the college). Different VLEs work in slightly different ways but the following are the more common features of relevance to assessment.

- **Storage of a range of resources to support learning. Tutors can store files, folders and pictures on VLEs for learners to access at a later date. It is also possible for tutors to track which learners use the VLE and when, and which files and folders are accessed by the learner.**
- **Establishment of an online discussion forum, sometimes called a virtual seminar. Sending and receiving emails is quick and easy but the scope for conversation is limited. By using an online**

discussion forum a genuine two-way dialogue can be facilitated. A VLE is not the only way to do this – other software is also available. Tutors can use a discussion forum to set learners a task for discussion, research and feedback, and monitor individual contributions as a form of formative assessment, in much the same way as a tutor would assess learning through contributions to a live seminar.

- Facilities for assessment activities such as quizzes, multiple-choice tests or short-answer responses. Learners can post their answers to assessment tasks through the VLE. Functions such as this are particularly useful for tutors of learners who only attend college on a part-time basis. Online activities such as this can help ensure a more structured approach to learning.

Computer networks

Normally, the computer systems in an institution are all linked to the same network. Any user, staff or learners, can log in to the network with a username and password. A network allows for files and folders to be swapped easily between computers, without needing to use removable storage media such as USB memory sticks or CDs. Networks all have a shared network drive, which is effectively a giant disk drive that all the users can access, and each user has a space on the network drive allocated to them for storing files and folders. On many networks, it is possible to set up a public folder that contains files and documents that are not protected by a password and that anyone with access to the network as a whole can use. A public folder offers some of the functionality of a VLE but with a lot less fuss. In order to use a VLE, learners – and tutors – need to get to know how the VLE works, how to operate its functions, how to manipulate the information within it, and so on. This can be off-putting for the computer novice. Accessing a network drive is very similar to accessing the hard drive on a stand-alone computer, however, and any tutor or learner who can open and use files and folders on a Windows-based computer will be able to access a public folder in a network drive.

The tutor can then set up the public drive in a number of ways. It may simply be a repository of useful files and documents from class, or it may contain resources that the learners will need to access and use for research, or any other kind of project, before the next session.

A cautionary note relating to ILT and e-assessment

ILT is not the universal panacea that some of its champions make out, however. The increased use of technology is a central part of current government action behind widening participation (for example, Learndirect) but recent research has highlighted some areas of concern.

The potential for distraction

We should not get enthused about ILT, and the potential for technology, at the expense of more basic, but no less important, learning and assessment strategies. A poorly-designed assignment will not be improved simply by including an element of ILT. For many learners and potential learners, ILT may prove to be a barrier to learning, not a conduit.

The misuse of technology

Simply loading information onto a VLE or to a network drive is no substitute for sequencing of learning and teaching. The potential to create a collection of resources is undoubtedly attractive but unless it is carefully structured and organised into appropriately sized components, learners may simply get lost while trying to navigate their way through the material.

The creation of new dilemmas for tutors and new problems for learners

The move towards e-learning and e-assessment has the potential to create new dilemmas for tutors to cope with. One example that has already received much attention is 'lurking'. During a seminar or group discussion, we often encounter learners who are unwilling or unable to participate in discussion, often for a variety of reasons. Lurking is the online equivalent, and refers to learners who log on to a group discussion site but do not participate.

Technological inequality

If we are to encourage learners to make more use of ILT, we need to remember that not all of them will enjoy the same access to technology outside the college. Internet-based research, for example, may be frustratingly slow without a high-speed internet connection, something that not all households have. Many households do not have internet access at all. Using public libraries may be one solution but this can be time-consuming and may involve travel or other expense. Learners can use college-based facilities, of course, but attending college outside class time may also be difficult.

A SUMMARY OF **KEY POINTS**

In this chapter, we have looked at the following key themes:

> **blended assessment and e-assessment;**

> **reasons for using ILT and potential pitfalls.**

There is a lot of political, as well as financial, capital encouraging the take-up of e-learning and e-assessment. The Department for Education and the Department for Business, Innovation and Skills both work to champion e-learning, and an increasingly large number of professional qualifications specialising in e-learning are now available. And at one level this is a good thing. But whilst a college-based tutor might have access to a well-equipped IT suite (although such equipment is far from evenly distributed), part-time community education tutors are often more concerned to ensure that there are enough tables and chairs, or that the heating has been left on. E-learning and e-assessment will not be appropriate for all learning and training contexts, but for many tutors working in larger institutions or formal education and training settings it is increasingly expected.

Branching options

Reflection

The adoption of ILT in teaching and learning is stressed by managers, awarding bodies and government ministers alike. Clearly, some curricula are more easily able to adopt a blended learning approach than others. So, before reflecting on how ILT might be used with your learners (and whether or not that would entail CPD on the part of the tutor!), consider the extent to which the subject that you teach can be supported by ILT in a meaningful and authentic way, rather than as an artificial 'bolt-on'.

Analysis

There are lots of reasons as to why ILT can and should be encouraged where appropriate, beyond the proliferation of education and training opportunities that are explicitly designed to improve IT skills. The use of IT is a part of everyday life for many, and as such it makes sense that further and adult education colleges should promote it. The teacher training qualification that you are currently working towards, or have recently completed, almost certainly requires IT skills. But do you think that all of the diverse learner groups within the Lifelong Learning sector need or want them?

Research

The suggestions for further reading cited below provide a small number of case studies for further research. Some of this research has been reported beyond the pages of academic journals, and has made it into the popular press. The use of interactive whiteboards in the classroom is a good example of an ILT initiative that has been promoted by government, and researched quite thoroughly. Carry out some web-based research, and evaluate the effectiveness of such interactive whiteboards. Find out how much they cost. Do you think the money could be better spent elsewhere?

REFERENCES AND FURTHER READING REFERENCES AND FURTHER READING

Beetham, H and Sharpe, R (eds.) (2007) *Rethinking Pedagogy for a Digital Age: designing and delivering e-learning*. Abingdon: Routledge.

Davis, M and Ralph, S (2001) 'Stalling the learning process: group dynamics in cyberspace' *Studies in the Education of Adults* 33,2.

Hill, C (2008) *Teaching with e-learning in the Lifelong Learning Sector*. Second edition. Exeter: Learning Matters.

Salmon, G (2003) *E-moderating: the key to teaching and learning on-line*. Second edition. London: RoutledgeFalmer.

Selwyn, N, Gorard, S and Furlong, J (2004) 'Adults Use of ICTs for Learning: reducing or increasing educational inequalities?' *Journal of Vocational Education and Training* 56,2.

Selwyn, N, Gorard, S and Williams, S (2002) ' "We are guinea pigs really": examining the realities of ICT based adult learning' *Studies in the Education of Adults* 34,1.

Appendix: Assessing and assuring the quality of assessment

In March 2010, new units of assessment, mapped onto the QCF, were published by Lifelong Learning UK relating to the role of workplace assessors. These qualifications, which map onto new national occupational standards (NOS) for workplace assessors, have effectively replaced the 'old' Assessor and Verifier awards ('A and V awards'). The new units of assessment have been written at National Qualifications Framework (NQF) levels 3 and 4, and are designed to complement the CertEd/PGCE/DTLLS curriculum. As such, and in the light of the fact that some CertEd/PGCE/DTLLS students also go on to work towards separate qualifications for the assessment of NVQs in the workplace, it is a worthwhile exercise to highlight those sections of this book that might usefully be used to support students in working towards these new awards, referred to by City and Guilds as Training, Assessment, Quality, Assurance (TAQA) awards. What follows, therefore, is a series of tables that map the contents of this book onto the learning outcomes (LOs) for each of the new units of assessment.

Unit one: understanding the principles and practices of assessment

LO1: Understand the principles and requirements of assessment	Chapters 1, 3, 4
LO2: Understand different types of assessment method	Chapter 5
LO3: Understand how to plan assessment	Chapter 1
LO4: Understand how to involve learners and others in assessment	Chapter 9
LO5: Understand how to make assessment decisions	Chapter 4
LO6: Understand quality assurance of the assessment process	Chapter 8
LO7: Understand how to manage information relating to assessment	Chapter 7
LO8: Understand the legal and good practice requirements in relation to assessment	Chapter 9

Unit two: assess occupational competence in the work environment

LO1: Be able to plan the assessment of occupational competence	Chapters 2, 3, 5
LO2: Be able to make assessment decisions about occupational competence	Chapters 2, 3, 5
LO3: Be able to provide required information following the assessment of occupational competence	Chapter 7
LO4: Be able to maintain legal and good practice requirements when assessing occupational competence	Chapter 9

Unit three: assess vocational skills, knowledge and understanding

LO1: Be able to prepare assessments of vocational skills, knowledge and understanding	Chapters 2, 5, 6
LO2: Be able to carry out assessments of vocational skills, knowledge and understanding	Chapters 2, 5, 6, 8
LO3: Be able to provide required information following the assessment of vocational skills, knowledge and understanding	Chapter 7
LO4: Be able to maintain legal and good practice requirements when assessing vocational skills, knowledge and understanding	Chapter 9

Unit four: understanding the principles and practices of internally assuring the quality of assessment

LO1: Understand the context and principles of internal quality assurance	Chapters 1, 8
LO2: Understand how to plan the internal quality assurance of assessment	Chapters 7, 8
LO3: Understand techniques and criteria for monitoring the quality of assessment internally	Chapters 4, 10
LO4: Understand how to internally maintain and improve the quality of assessment	Chapters 4, 6
LO5: Understand how to manage information relevant to the internal quality assurance of assessment	Chapter 7
LO6: Understand the legal and good practice requirements for the internal quality assurance of assessment	Chapter 9

Unit five: internally assure the quality of assessment

LO1: Be able to plan the internal quality assurance of assessment	Chapter 8
LO2: Be able to internally evaluate the quality of assessment	Chapters 4, 8
LO3: Be able to internally maintain and improve the quality of assessment	Chapter 8
LO4: Be able to manage information relevant to the internal quality assurance of assessment	Chapter 7
LO5: Be able to maintain legal and good practice requirements when internally moderating and maintaining the quality of assessment	Chapter 9

Unit six: understanding the principles and practices of externally assuring the quality of assessment

LO1: Understand the context and principles of external quality assurance	Chapters 1, 8
LO2: Understand how to plan the external quality assurance of assessment	Chapter 8
LO3: Understand how to externally evaluate the quality of assessment and internal quality assurance	Chapters 1, 4, 8
LO4: Understand how to externally maintain and improve the quality of assessment	Chapter 8
LO5: Understand how to manage information relevant to external quality assurance	Chapter 7
LO6: Understand the legal and good practice requirements relating to external quality assurance	Chapters 7, 9

Unit seven: externally assure the quality of assessment

LO1: Be able to plan the external quality assurance of assessment	Chapters 1, 8
LO2: Be able to externally evaluate internal quality assurance and assessment	Chapters 4, 8
LO3: Be able to maintain and improve internal quality assurance processes	Chapter 8
LO4: Be able to manage information relevant to the external quality assurance of assessment	Chapter 7
LO5: Be able to maintain legal and good practice requirements when externally monitoring and maintaining the quality of assessment	Chapter 9

Unit eight: plan, allocate and monitor work in own area of responsibility

LO1: Be able to produce a work plan for own area of responsibility	Chapter 1
LO2: Be able to allocate and agree responsibilities with team members	Chapter 1
LO3: Be able to monitor the progress and quality of work in own area of responsibility and provide feedback	Chapter 8
LO4: Be able to review and amend plans of work for own area of responsibility and communicate changes	Chapters 7, 8

Index